Before you dive into my
CONCLUSIONS
Pragmatic Reality

In Search of Secular Ethics
It seems only fair that you get some idea why.
Hence a word or two about my:

DELUSIONS
Pragmatic Realism

Stanislaw Kapuscinski advances compelling arguments regarding *DELUSIONS* ingrained and perpetrated by both, the religious and the scientific communities. He concludes that science/religion arguments are equally as deluded on both sides of the equation, particularly when advanced from the pre-eminently fundamentalist point of view.

Some blurbs from 5-Star reviews on Amazon:

Excellent!
Splendidly written!
Much to think about!
Intriguing and very brave!
Well deserving of a 5-star rating!
Well written and a fantastic read!
A mind-expanding philosophical joy ride!
I Love It When You Discover a Book Like This!!

While Richard Dawkins motivated me to write
DELUSIONS—Pragmatic Realism,
Dalai Lama's search for Secular Ethics influenced my
CONCLUSIONS—Pragmatic Reality

CONCLUSIONS
Pragmatic Reality

Stanisław Kapuściński

PUBLISHED BY INHOUSEPRESS

Copyright © 2020 by Stanislaw Kapuscinski
Paperback Edition 2020

All rights reserved. No part of this publication may be reproduced or transmitted in any form or by any means electronic, mechanical, photocopying, recording or otherwise, without the prior written permission of the publisher.

ISBN 978-1-987864-32-8

For my wife
Bozena Happach
The Sculptor
who inspires me to appreciate the illusive beauty
of the
Phenomenal World

Christmas
2019

Contents

FOREWORD to *DELUSIONS*
FOREWORD to *CONCLUSIONS*
INTRODUCTION

PART ONE — PAST
(In parenthesis are the titles of chapters in *DELUSIONS—Pragmatic Realism*, which I endeavour to comment on and answer in ***CONCLUSIONS—Pragmatic Reality***)

Chapter 1	21
WHO IS RIGHT? (Fundamentalism ...)	
Chapter 2	31
IT'S ALL UP TO US (Where We Were)	
Chapter 3	40
HERMAPHRODITES (What We Were)	
Chapter 4	57
METAMORPHOSIS (The God Diffusion)	
Chapter 5	65
MANY ARE CALLED (The Beginning and the End)	
Chapter 6	74
EDUCATION (Why We Were)	
Essay #52—*Beyond Religion I*	
Chapter 7	79
CAUSE & EFFECT (Atheist's Delusion)	

PART TWO — PRESENT

Chapter 8	87
KNOWLEDGE (Fundamentalism in Religion and Science)	
Chapter 9	91
AGE OF AQUARIUS (Where We Are)	
Chapter 10	99
BEING & BECOMING (What We Are)	
Chapter 11	111
ALL IS ENERGY (The God Diffusion)	
Chapter 12	115
KNOWLEDGE WITHIN (The End of the Beginning)	

Chapter 13   118
TIME (Why We Are: Phase Two) [Also read Appendix IV]
Chapter 14   131
MISUNDERSTOOD DELUSION? (Atheist's Delusion)

PART THREE — FUTURE

Chapter 15   139
DOGMATIC MISUNDERSTANDING
(Fundamentalism in Religion and Science)
Chapter 16   144
GRATITUDE (Where We Might Be)
Chapter 17   153
WE REALLY ARE GODS (What We Might Be)
Chapter 18   171
PHENOMENAL DIFFUSION (The God Diffusion)
Chapter 19   176
THE NEW DAWN (The Beginning of the End)
Chapter 20   184
INVETERATE DUALITY (Why We Shall Be: Phase Three)
Chapter 21   203
GOOD, EVIL & IMMORTALITY (Scientist's Delusion)

~~~~~~

POSTSCRIPTUM

APPENDIX I   231
THE PRESENT (The Church)
Incl. Essay #18 — *Beyond Religion III*
APPENDIX II   240
THE ESSENCE OF DIVERSITY (Science)
APPENDIX III   246
THE INCONVENIENT TRUTH
APPENDIX IV   261
ESSENCE OF LIFE
EPILOGUE   264

BIBLIOGRAPHY   275
A word about the Author

FOREWORD to *DELUSIONS*

I am reminded of a story *about a seeker, a man from the West, coming upon two Buddhist monks. They were sitting in a contemplative silence, some distance apart. After waiting for a respectful while, in an attempt to understand the Infinite, the tourist asked the first monk,*

"Is there a God?"

The monk opened his eyes, looked with patient tolerance at the traveler and replied, "Of course not."

The seeker shook his head in deep disappointment. Yet, the scientific part of his brain smiled with satisfaction. On the other hand, having been trained in the scientific method he felt a deep void in his heart. His upbringing and training precluded the existence of the permanent; of something he could fall back on if all else failed, and in science things changed constantly—even the universe. But, he was a seeker; he refused to give up. After another while he approached the second monk and repeated the same question,

"Is there a God?"

The second monk opened his eyes, looked at the traveler with inherent compassion and replied, "Of course. I am."

It sounded like a Zen Koan. Or, in Master Hyakujo's words, "The enlightened man is one with causation."

The seeker remembered: "The perceiver and the perceived are one."

Contented, the seeker went on his way.

FOREWORD to *CONCLUSIONS*

For me it all began in 1948. I was sixteen then. Garry Davis was much older. On May 25th that year he walked into the American Embassy in Paris, renounced his American citizenship, and declared himself a Citizen of the World.

I had no citizenship to renounce. I left Poland illegally and by 1948 arrived in England as the son of a Polish officer, who was already an active member of the Polish Second Corps, affiliated to the British army. I was a displaced person already, without any citizenship. However, wanting to hitchhike to the south of France, I needed a passport.

To cut the story short, I also declared myself a Citizen of the World. However, as with Garry Davis, no one listened. I had been given a bilingual "Travel Document", also known as *"Titre de Voyage"*, and I hitchhiked to Mandelieu, on the French Riviera, feeling free and easy. Furthermore, the experience left me with a nagging need for absolute freedom.

Next came a book on Yoga. A few months later I felt sure I had been levitating a foot or so above the floor while meditating. Seventy years later Einstein confirmed that all is illusion, yet... *very* persistent one.

I have been persisting ever since.

I began questioning the reality of the phenomenal world I lived in. Miracles became subject of scientific study, not of religious superstitions. Quantum Theory is just beginning to catch up with the understanding of reality of the great masters of the past.

I'm still working on it.

As for the world at large, not much has changed. The Buddhist monks still sit in a contemplative silence. They still ponder the Infinite within and without them. Another man from the West asked the same question as his predecessor did some years ago:

"Is there a God?"

The monk turned his dreamy eyes at the tourist.

"Define what you mean by God."

The tourist was stumped. Didn't Baruch Spinoza once say that: "To define God is to deny God"? Of course, to define means to limit, and if you limit God, then He'd no longer be God. At least, not the Almighty One. *He*, that's already a limitation. Perhaps *He*'s a *She*. Or a *Hermaphrodite*? Or not even human at all?

Well, maybe the Greeks were right. Who could tell what billions of years would evolve? Maybe there are many gods.

"Never mind," the tourist said. He didn't want to place limitations on the Unlimited.

The monk smiled knowingly.

INTRODUCTION

> *"In nature there are neither rewards nor punishments; there are consequences."*
> **Robert Green Ingersoll (1833—1899)**
> American social activist, orator and agnostic

> *"The good man is the friend of all living things."*
> **Mahatma Gandhi**
> Indian lawyer and political ethicist

> "Sometimes legends make reality, and become more useful than the facts."
> **Salman Rushdie**
> Author

While not adhering to the Content page of *DELUSIONS* to the letter, I shall endeavour to follow the general intent of the book in order not to leave any questions unanswered. My ***CONCLUSIONS*** to the questions raised will be more concise, resembling essays, on the subjects raised in my previous book. To facilitate continuity, each new chapter title is followed by the previous one in ***DELUSIONS***. Whenever possible, my intention is not to leave any questions unanswered. Nevertheless, I have no wish to impose my conclusions on other people's ideas. After all, we were all born to contribute to the diversity of the Universe. More about this later.

The whole of the present dissertation is based on three premises:

1. Albert Einstein's assurance and that:
"All is Energy",
2. That:
"Reality is merely an illusion,
albeit a very persistent one."
and:
3. The biblical statement:
"Ye are gods."

To once again use Einstein's expression: *"The rest are details."*

I shall no longer pretend to follow, even euphemistically, in Richard Dawkins's illustrious footsteps. Any man who purports that the phenomenal Universe 'happened' out of nothing, or even out of a 'Big Bang', does not deserve to be taken seriously. On the other hand, I do like his sense of humour. Anything he does not understand, he deems to be nonsense — like the Bible, which he (as well as all people who wish to use it to control people's minds, behaviour, and pocket) regards as a religious document, whereas in fact it has nothing whatsoever to do with any religion.

> *The Bible is no less and no more than a compendium of knowledge, compiled over countless centuries, which defines human potential, and suggests how to lead a happy life. Hence, it teaches us how to create our own phenomenal reality.*

Yet, over many centuries, it has been usurped by various religious factions and used as a carrot and a stick to control those of weaker minds, or even just softer hearts.

Heaven — Extreme carrot.

Hell — Extreme stick.

In the spring of 1949, a mere few years after WW2, Jack Wyrtzen and Percy Crawford switched from radio to **TV** broadcasting. Another television preacher of note was Fulton J. Sheen, who successfully switched to **TV** in 1951 after two decades of popular radio broadcasts. *Time* Magazine called him, erroneously, the *first televangelist*. However, in those early days, TV preachers weren't, as yet, multimillionaires flying their multimillion-dollar private jets to generate more money. Gradually greed has set in. The carrot and the stick have been supplemented by offers of salvation for a few weekly dollars.

Don't get me wrong: there are a few *bona fide* saints emerging from religious communities. Very few... and very many "*ersatz* saints" who had been canonized for political purposes. Just like the Nobel Prize.

While I still admire Mr. Dawkins's predisposition to praise the literary merits of the King James Bible of 1611 (while ignoring its content), I do wish he'd stop deluding himself that he has any idea what the Bible is about. For that one needs at least an elementary knowledge of symbolism, of which he is sadly bereft. He might find my *DICTIONARY OF BIBLICAL SYMBOLISM* of some help.

By contrast, or tacit agreement, the rest of our illustrious scientists continue to treat the Universe as an enormous conglomerate of planets, stars and galaxies, all material objects, completely ignoring the brighter minds amongst them who reached the conclusion sometime ago, that:

ALL IS ENERGY.

Not only that all matter could be *converted* to energy as in $E=mc^2$ but, as an example, that a hydrogen atom that consists of 99.9999999999996% empty space, the infinitely small nucleus, or the remainder of what is recognized as atom, is still energy. We live and learn. Or some of us do...

> *In the theory of gravity, physicists often discuss a **point mass**, meaning a point particle with a nonzero mass and no other properties or structure. Likewise, in electromagnetism, physicists discuss a **point charge**, a point particle with a nonzero charge.*
> (Wikipedia. "Point particle")[1]

This might have been the reason why Einstein suspected that phenomenal reality is an illusion.

The point I am making is that, in an atom, 'matter' content is so small that we do not have adequate units of measurement that could adequately describe them. The best we can say is they are more than "nothing" but... hardly so. They are merely *points at which certain energies are concentrated.*

And yet...

And yet stars, and galaxies, and the whole enormity of the ever-expanding Universe is made of them.

And then, in 1927, Louis de Broglie demonstrated the wave-like behaviour of (nonzero mass) particles which became the basis of quantum mechanics, which also, to this day, manages to confuse even the best brains in the scientific community.

Louis de Broglie was followed by Max Planck, Erwin Schrodinger, Max Born, Werner Heisenberg, Paul Dirac, Niels Bohr, not to mention our dear old Albert Einstein. Finally, Richard Feynman, together with Shin'ichiro Tomonaga and Julian Schwinger, have been awarded the Nobel Prize for *"their fundamental work in quantum electrodynamics, with deep-ploughing consequences for the physics of elementary particles."*

CONCLUSIONS

Having been awarded the Nobel Prize, Richard Feynman publically assured us that:

"It is safe to say that no one understands Quantum Mechanics."

I am delighted to belong to such an illustrious fraternity of famous, ignorant scientists. I, too, am bereft of understanding.

And this brings us, more or less, up to date. We are all ignorant. Not because we're all mentally deficient, only because the Universe is stranger than we can, as yet, imagine. This last opinion also belongs to Richard Feynman.

Don't you just love honest people, let alone honest scientists?

While I do not blame Richard Dawkins for anything within the field of his expertise, I do hold his namesake, Richard Feynman directly responsible for my drifting into the field of metaphysics.

Science was, for me, no longer enough. While I continued to admire it as a method for procuring knowledge of the phenomenal Universe, it left me wanting for results. Also, it tended to ignore the elusive, illusionary character of reality, such as promulgated by Albert Einstein.

As mentioned, science is intended to be a method, not an answer to all the unknowns. Science produces theories which are taken as working hypotheses, until a better theory makes the unknowns just a tad clearer. Just a tad. There is no hurry. We have eternity to find the answers, and by then, the questions will have changed.

That's the beauty of metaphysics. It reaches beyond physics. Beyond what is. It reaches into the field of what could, or might be.

To be quite honest, even after I started jotting down notes on material for **CONCLUSIONS—*Pragmatic Reality***, I had only a vague idea what I was going to write. What I did do, however, was to double the time I allotted to contemplation. I'd relax in a prone position, close my eyes, try my best to eliminate any external detractions— and wait. Within a week I began to see where I was going. Within two weeks I started writing.

And then, one day, it came to me.

Finally, I had a clear idea what this book was going to be about. Conclusions, yes, but what conclusions—that was the point. On Thursday, October 31st, 2019, I saw the Universe in all its glory. Gradually I shall unfold my vision to you. The only surprising thing I discovered was that the mystery, the secret of the *"thoughts of God"* (to use Einstein's expression), has been unfolded to us thousands of years ago. Only our pride, our egos, and perhaps our greed, stopped us from assuming the humble role which we are destined to play here, on Earth, in this phenomenal reality.

On the other hand, our purpose is so magnificent that we did not dare to face the truth.

Well, now we must.

The Age of Aquarius demands it of us. We must stop leaning on, relying on, and blaming our leaders for our successes and failures. We must take our rightful place in the scheme of things. In the infinity of the Universe. In the infinity of time.

We must grow up.

(1) A Point Charge is an electric charge regarded as concentrated in a mathematical point, without spatial extent.

PART ONE — THE PAST

"...all matter originates and exists only by virtue of a force which brings the particles of an atom to vibration which holds the atom together. We must assume behind this force is the existence of a conscious and intelligent mind.
This mind is the matrix of all matter."
Max Planck (1858—1947)
Nobel Prize in Physics in 1918

"Reality is merely an illusion, although a very persistent one."
Albert Einstein (1879 –1955)
Nobel Prize in Physics in 1921

Chapter 1
WHO IS RIGHT?
(Fundamentalism in Religion and Science).

> *A fanatic is a man who consciously overcompensates a secret doubt.*
> **Aldous Leonard Huxley (1894—1963)**
> British author

> *"If you wish to understand the universe, think of energy, frequency and vibration."*
> **Nikola Tesla (1856 – 1943)**
> Serbian-American inventor, electrical engineer, mechanical engineer, and futurist

As I've suggested in my *DELUSIONS—Pragmatic Realism*, fundamentalists are always right. Be they of religious persuasion, or steeped in scientific jargon, they are always right.

For thousands of years, some very wise people attempted to break into the mystery of the Universal Laws. Those running religions called them dogmas; the scientific authorities referred to them as... facts. On the other hand, many saints, mystics, even Saviours[1] (there may have been 16 of them) as well as noted scientists, tried to know, let alone understand, what Einstein called *"the thoughts of God"*. *"The rest are details,"* he'd said.

And, in a way, he was right.

The problem is, however, that in the phenomenal reality all details count. Atoms, subatomic particles such as electrons, protons, quarks... they all count. Even waves count. Do they have anything to do with the thoughts of

God? Well, this depends by who or what we mean by 'God'.

And yet, though neither group would admit it, both religious and scientific communities continue to try to make sense of the phenomenal reality, while supposedly realizing that it is only an illusion.

Why?

At long last Albert Einstein supplied us with an answer. Because, he said:

ALL IS ENERGY.

The 'visible' universe might be constructed of (supposedly) 'solid' particles, such as atoms, but, in fact, atoms are no more than energy vibrating at a very slow rate. Till now we recognized movement mostly by changing localities of matter. Now we have to look at staying in the same location, but vibrating at different rates.

One might have thought that this single statement would put to sleep the eternal struggle between "mind and faith".

Not so.

It not only didn't provide an answer but, instead of defining what might be the thoughts of God, we now had to decide: what is energy.

Back to square one.

Though... not quite.

First, let us define what we mean by vibration. In scientific terms, it refers to transducer which metamorphoses energy. Originally it was merely:

> *"a device that converts variations in a physical quantity, such as pressure or brightness, into an electrical signal, or vice versa."* [2]

Today we accept that a transducer can convert one form

of energy into another, essentially by changing its rate of vibration.

Our built-in transducer is not of phenomenal construction. It consists of the energy of Consciousness. What makes this energy different from all the other energies is that it is omnipresent and hence it vibrates at an infinite rate. It is to our thought processes what air is to our lungs. In fact when reduced to the very first principle, we are individualizations of the Omnipresent Energy of Consciousness, after millions of years of metamorphoses.

Consciousness is also an omnipresent Transducer.

That's it.

No more and no less, although...

...although Consciousness requires a subsidiary mechanism to actually affect changes in phenomenal reality. We refer to that mechanism as *mind*, which is not to be confused with brain. More on this subject later.

[There seem to be exceptions, however. A study published recently shows that whole-body vibration could offer an alternative to exercise in the fight against obesity and diabetes.] Good luck!

However, there is a fly in this ointment. While we abide in this phenomenal reality, the evolutionary process of the creative energy of Consciousness has resulted in a complex biological computer known as brain. This electrochemical system is capable of producing artificial intelligence. Some 100 billion neurons are also working overtime to keep us alive. They communicate with each other by firing electrochemical impulses between 5 and 50 times every second across the junction between two nerve cells. The neurons in excess of those necessary for our survival can be used to produce artificial intelligence.

According to Wikipedia:

> *"Each individual neuron can form thousands of links with other neurons (and) in this way, giving a typical **brain** well over 100 trillion **synapses** (up to 1,000 trillion, by some estimates.)* [3]

This AI (Artificial Intelligence) serves to produce consciousness, which manifests as Ego. While Ego creates diversity by keeping us separate from each other as well as from the rest of the Universe, it is indispensible for the transient survival of our phenomenal bodies.

When our individualized Consciousness leaves our physical enclosures, the artificial consciousness is often in sufficient rapport with the 'real' consciousness, to survive (not lose its individuality) until the next embodiment in the phenomenal reality, often referred to as reincarnation.

Recently, German and Greek scientists discovered a new form of brain activity even more powerful than previously imagined. The activities of *'dendrites'*[4] at the end of neurons appear to show that a single neuron is capable of solving computational problems without involving other neurons. The co-author of the study, Matthew Larkum, a neuroscientist at Humboldt University of Berlin,[5] wrote:

> *"The dendrites are central to understanding the brain because they are at the core of what determines the computational power of single neurons. There was a 'eureka' moment when we saw the dendritic action potentials for the first time,"*

We live and learn.

It seems that Evelyn Monahan really was right when she claimed that we are: *"magnificent human beings... without equal in all creation,"* (See Chapter 3), although the activities of dendrites have not, as yet, been studied in other species.

And, after all, others have laid claim, millennia ago, that we are gods! Or are we, as Einstein has said, but an illusion?

So... who is right?

I question both, the religious and the scientific theories. It is likely that each one of us must define reality for ourselves. After all, we are *individualizations* of the Omnipresent Consciousness. Yet there is a strange, for me irresistible, boon to my conclusions. My philosophy not only assures me of immortality, but enables me to abide, here on Earth, in the antechamber of Heaven, which is little less than Paradise. And then it leads to a temporary haven, or perhaps Heaven, of *Devachan* (which will be explained in Chapter 2).

There is one more item for us to consider.

Some neuroscientists claim that it is not the number of neurons but that the synaptic activity is the source of our intelligence. This may be true of the AI generated by the electrochemical entanglement, but we must never forget that the 'real' intelligence is derived from the Omnipresent Consciousness, the individualization of which uses our brain as a biological computer to create an effect in the phenomenal reality. Also, considering the number of neurons and the resulting synapses, (not to mentions the recent discovery of the dendritic activity), and comparing the diversity they produce, it seems more than probable that we use only a minute portion of our brain's capacity.

Do we need every synapse that fires in our brain?

Consider the countless years of evolution. Let us assume that only the brains produce diversity in the phenomenal Universe. (After all, what else? A Big Juju sitting on a cloud some billions of light-years away?) Then consider the diversity already created, and think of the next million years or two.

And then think of eternity.

Eternity takes us inexorably towards cyclic evolution. While a few million years might suffice to construct a human body, eternity must have been responsible for many such efforts to account for the present enormous size and complexity of the phenomenal Universe. Measuring the size of it in time, the distance between Earth and the edge of the observable Universe is 46 billion light-years, making the diameter of the observable Universe around 93 billion light-years. This is billions of years before any human has been thought of, even by the Omnipresent Consciousness. On the other hand, beyond the reality of the phenomenal Universe there is no time. There is only the eternal Present. Hence, we must have existed in our potential form billions of years before Adam and Eve thought of tasting the apple.

One can but wonder what our predecessors might have been like. By now, compared to us, they must seem like gods.

Remember our myths...?

Back to AI. The 100 billion neurons communicate with each other, producing complex answers to simple questions.[5] However AI, although it is a product of the phenomenal reality, is just as elusive, as illusory, as the rest of our reality. The prime purpose of our brain is to keep us (temporarily) alive and well. But then there are those extra neurons dedicated to a 'higher' purpose.

And here comes a great surprise. What of those extra neurons dedicated to a 'higher' purpose?

Very few people know how to use their biological computer *consciously* to produce phenomenal results. Very few of us realize that the assembly of neurons is capable of producing an illusion of countless galaxies, let alone our own, magnificent, no matter how transient, physical bodies. Our bodies consisting of trillions of cells.

The mind, not the brain, generates ideas. Ideas that originate in the Eternal Present of the Omnipresent Consciousness.

The brain (the biological computer) converts them into thoughts. Thoughts, when generated through the alpha brainwaves create significant illusions in our phenomenal reality. The reality that we recognize as real, although, as we already know, Einstein insists that they are *"merely an illusion, although a very persistent one."*

The rest is history, except for a pertinent detail.
We forgot to discuss how it all began.
Well — it didn't.
Creativity is a process that is inherent to our awareness of the reality in which we find our becoming. But as every child must have parents, so our awareness must have originated from an non-phenomenal source. The source, which religionists call God and scientists call *"nothing which existed before the Big Bang"*. I prefer the first option, though not one created in the image of man.

Let us go back to Albert Einstein. We can take his words, or the words of a dozen televangelists and suchlike. Einstein said that ALL IS ENERGY. Hence that which the sacerdotal fraternity refer to as God, must, per force also be Energy. All means ALL. No exclusions. ALL must also include the potential energy that was, is, will be or could be, though not in its phenomenal form. Thus we must expand our concept of ENERGY to include EVERYTHING. Energy that was, is, will be or could be.

Eternal, hence "inexhaustible Energy"?

There are only a few adjectives that do not diminish or

limit the definition of God that even Baruch Spinoza would accept:

Omnipresent, Eternal, Inexhaustible Energy, Infinite Potential...

And to this impressive list we must add the most magnificent definition of energy of them all:

CREATIVE CONSCIOUSNESS

Or, to be more precise, ***the energy*** **of the Creative Consciousness**. This, and this alone, does not diminish or restrict the religious concept of God.

This definition, however, opens the gates to include thoughts and emotions in the concept of energies. They are the two elements necessary to fulfill the creative process. Perhaps, in time, we shall discover others, such as love, hate, faith... they all produce phenomenal consequences, hence they can be classified as energies.

Before time began *i.e.,* before the first manifestation of the Infinite Potential (if there ever was such a time), the Omnipresent Consciousness must have created the phenomenal reality through trial and error. At some stage of eternity, the Potential Energy of the Omnipresent Consciousness must have chosen to individualize Itself, *in order to create phenomenal diversity*. Or, it always had some degree of manifestation of phenomenality (think of our dreams), but only when evolutionary process created artificial intelligence the consequent diversity resulted in the Universe we enjoy today.

Who knows what the next few billions of years will produce? The ongoing expansion will take us towards infinity that cannot be reached...

As someone has said, the Universe is likely to be stranger than we can imagine.

Isn't it already?

This ongoing inherent need for diversity is responsible for the continuous expansion of the phenomenal Universe. As the population (on Earth and elsewhere?) increases, the expansion accelerates.

Once the phenomenal manifestations persisted for a significant duration, time was born. Contrary to popular belief, the Omnipresent Consciousness continues to generate ideas which produce the phenomenal illusions which we recognize as the material Universe.

As the Potential is infinite, this is an ONGOING PROCESS.

This leads me to conclude that some version of AI must have existed before the present phenomenal Universe became perceptible to our senses. We can only retreat to ancient myths which have gradually devolved into religions.

Of one thing we can be fairly certain. The Egos of even our more famous men and women are likely to be wrong. The Self, the "Higher Self", the individualization of the Omnipresent Consciousness is always right. It always guides us towards increasing the diversity and enhancing the Universe—our transient Paradise.

Or... the phenomenal Universe would have long ceased to exist. Aren't we lucky?

~~~

(1) Wikipedia quotes from a book by Kersey Graves,
https://en.wikipedia.org/wiki/The_World%27s_Sixteen_Crucified_Saviors
"The World's Sixteen Crucified Saviors":
Thulis of Egypt, 1700 B. C.
Krishna of India, 1200 B.C.
Crite of Chaldea, 1200 B.C.
Atys of Phrygia, 1170 B.C.
Thammuz or Tammuz of Syria, 1160 B.C.

Hesus or Eros 834 B.C.
Bali of Orissa, 725 B.C.
Indra of Thibet (Tibet), 725 B.C.
Iao of Nepaul (Nepal), 622 B.C.
Buddha Sakia (Muni) of India, 600 B.C.
Mitra (Mithra) of Persia, 600 B.C.
Alcestos of Euripides, 600 B.C.
Quezalcoatl of Mexico, 587 B.C.
Wittoba of the Bilingonese, 552 B.C.
Prometheus or Æschylus of Caucasus, 547 B.C.
Quirinus of Rome, 506 B.C.

(2) from Latin *transducere* 'lead across' (from *trans-* 'across' + *ducere* 'lead') + -er.

(3) https://human-memory.net › brain-neurons-synapses
The calculations have been reputedly done by Suzana Herculano - Houzel, a Brazilian neuroscientist, has reduced this number of neurons to a 'mere' to 86 billion, though no mention was made whose brain she was measuring.

(4) Short branched extensions of a nerve cell, along which impulses received from other cells at synapses are transmitted to the cell body. (Google)

(5) A lot more info on Mathew Larkum's work below:
https://scholar.google.ca/citations?user=xFT6dFgAAAAJ&hl=en

Chapter 2
IT'S ALL UP TO US
(Where We Were)

> *Do what you can, with what you have, where you are.*
> **Theodore Roosevelt, (1858 - 1919)**
> 26th US President

> *"If it weren't for painting, I wouldn't live;
> I couldn't bear the extra strain of things."*
> **Winston Churchill**
> Wartime Prime Minister of Great Britain

> *"Do every act of your life as if it were your last."*
> **Marcus Aurelius (121 -180)**
> Roman Emperor and Stoic philosopher.

As you've read in *DELUSIONS* in 2012, according to the still functioning Flat Earth Society the Earth is still flat. Since I've written about it, I discovered that in November 2019:

> *"Brazil hosted a flat Earth conference... in Sao Paulo. In fact, this wasn't even the first flat Earth conference to have taken place internationally, with last year's gatherings in Birmingham, UK, Denver, Colorado and Edmonton, Alberta suggesting that flat Earthism is becoming quite the cultural phenomenon."*

(From an article by Simon Chandler,

a London-based journalist focusing on politics and technology).

You can read my comments about this group of 'scientists' in *DELUSIONS*. Don't forget that our Earth is, according to Einstein, an illusion, hence any shape might be acceptable. For now, I invite you on a more philosophically inclined journey.

As you must have seen in the prequel to this book, some peoples' brains are flatter than others. Or, perhaps, they are just illusory? If you hadn't yet read ***"DELUSIONS— Pragmatic Realism,"*** read it now. Please. Don't delay!

It's all there.

Moving even further back, in fact back for countless years, probably countless millennia if not millions of years, we imagined that we live on Earth for no particular reason, other than to survive for as long as we could. This, after all, seems to be the principal preoccupation of other species, of other animals, who, to our knowledge, have not yet begun to create their own, artificial realities. They love one another, and only attack, let alone eat each other to preserve their lives. We, humans, often kill for fun. To collect trophies.

To bolster of our Egos.

(To get disgustingly fat?)

And then came the mystics, the prophets, and even messiahs. They, until recently, have been the only ones, the only true scientists, who suggested that we are more than flesh and bones; that we can create realities which we can 'persistently pretend' to be real. They also suggested that life on Earth is not the only form of existence, but rather a transient stage of becoming, after which we shall move, upon 'dying' (vacating our illusory bodies), to a 'higher' reality.

A reality that manifests at a higher rate of vibrations.

CONCLUSIONS 33

(But this understanding came much later.)

Those ideas were summarily exploited by men who created religions, for the sole purpose of controlling people's minds. For what other nefarious reason they did so, we shall leave for now.

Or... let us come clean.

Even today, a number of religious leaders tend to live in unprecedented luxury compared to those whose minds they control. In the past, they had been directly responsible for creating, installing, and protecting countless architectural, sculptural, and painting treasures, which to this day we recognize as works of art, and that often served as inspiration for wonderful compositions of music. And then TV took over and their contribution of art was over. Dead. They built palaces for themselves, instead.

As you can see, there is a reason for everything.

The reason for the opulence of the TV *evangelists* may be to show "simple folk" (The *Third Party*) the transiency of greed. I strongly suspect that history will soon forget their extravagances, while those endowed with humility will endure the test of time. We can count them among the artists, composers, mystics, not to mention the Messiah. Few if any of them were ever rich.

And then, finally, came Albert Einstein who, with a single sentence, upset the philosophical, religious and even practical apple cart. I feel I must keep repeating his words:

"*Reality is merely an illusion, albeit a very persistent one.*"

So much for life on Earth.

Flat or otherwise. Unless...

Unless the only purpose of life on Earth is to prepare, if not create, an individualized state of consciousness in which we may want to spend extended periods of time. Some Mahatmas[1] claim that the stages between reincarnations in this 'valley of tears' can last, on average, 1500 years.

Hence, most of us, having done relatively little, don't retire to "rest in peace" *i.e.,* to do nothing forever after. We don't retire to exist eternally in a state of abysmal boredom usually referred to as Heaven. Instead, it seems, that we take a protracted holiday in **Devachan**, a temporary abode which:

> *"...is regarded as the place where most souls go after death where desires are gratified, corresponding to the Christian belief in Heaven. However, Devachan is a temporary intermediate state of being before the soul's eventual rebirth into the physical world."*

(H.P. Blavatsky, *The Theosophical Glossary*. Theosophical Publishing Society, 1892, page 98)

To support this thesis, a verse from St. Paul's 2nd letter to Corinthians[2] comes to mind: *"I know a man in Christ who was caught up to the* **third heaven***..."* As you can see, Blavatsky wasn't just making things up.

Let us make sure that we do not confuse *Devachan* with the Christian version of Purgatory, which is far, far more unpleasant state of consciousness than *Devachan*. While *Devachan* can be a stint wherein we are rewarded for having created an existence of joy and pleasure, the Purgatory is said to be a purely punitive condition. According to Christian doctrine we are not sent there as a reward, but as punishment. As cleansing process, at best. After all, Christianity has long forsaken Yeshûa's teaching, and has built a "carrot and the stick philosophy" with the absolutes of Heaven and Hell as unchangeable, irrevocable, permanent states of consciousness. Purgatory is supposed to be only a way station for a cleanup before a permanent entry to Heaven.

Even the word 'sin', has changed its meaning. It originates from Greek sport of archery. The word *hamartia*, (although later assumed to mean "*a fatal flaw leading to the downfall of a tragic hero or heroine*"), is translated as **sin** in the KJV and other versions of the Bible. Actually, in the sport of archery, it means *"missing the mark."*

Hardly a reason for eternal hellfire.

Alas, some of us prefer to believe in the Christ's teaching, and not in the perverted version of it promulgated by the sacerdotal fraternities. After all, the Christ said that ***"Kingdom of God is within you."***[3] We must assume that Kingdom of God is as close to Heaven as we can get.

Nevertheless, H.P. Blavatsky, purporting the thesis of theosophy, assures us that:

> *"Through Wisdom and Knowledge, one can reach Nirvana and be free from the cycle of birth and death, and even the "false bliss" of Devachan.*
> (H.P. Blavatsky, the *Secret Doctrine*)

We wouldn't be able to verify if the bliss of *Devachan* is real, unless we'd been there. There are, however, a number of people throughout history who have strong recollections of previous lives. Even Yeshûa (the original name of Jesus in case you've forgotten) asked his followers, *"Who do people say I am?"*[4] And the responses implied a wide-spread belief in reincarnation, suggesting that Yeshûa was, or might be, the return of John the Baptist, or Elijah, Jeremiah, or one of the prophets.[5] And yet, most religionists cannot find evidence for reincarnation in the Bible. It is quite amazing how blind are all who insist on leading the blind.

On the other hand, we cannot confirm Blavatsky's thesis as, to my knowledge, no one has yet achieved "absolute

Wisdom and Knowledge" and has since then returned to Earth to bear witness that she was right.

As for life on Earth, it all sounds fairly promising until, once again, we recall Einstein. As our phenomenal reality apparently is no more than an illusion, it seems that we are creating it with our minds, with our thoughts and desires, and eventually with our resulting actions. We, and we alone, create "realities" which we regard as real.

Beauty for one, is mundane for another.

Riches for some, is near poverty for another.

Physical possessions for one, are but irons restricting freedom for another.

Even peaceful happiness of one is a state of boredom for some.

And so forth. It all seems subjective.

I'd suggest that the only purpose of our life in this illusory reality of the phenomenal Earth is to practice and prepare our consciousness for extended periods we are about to spend in Devachan. After all, 1500 years might be regarded as eternity by some who have created realities which, at a higher rate of vibration of Devachan, might have no value at all. Reality that might no more resemble Heaven than the Christian Purgatory.

Like everything else in the phenomenal realities (subjective?) times between reincarnations vary. Theosophy offers the following:

> *According to Helena P. Blavatsky, the average span **between** lives (on Earth) is 1,000 to 1,500 years. The more mature and spiritual the person is, the longer is the "rest" period in DEVACHAN. Plato, for example, who lived 2,500 years ago, is said to be not reincarnated yet.*

Other sources define the average time between incarnations as 5 years at the primitive stage, 300 years at the civilized stage, 1000 years at the developed stage, 1500 years at the humanistic stage, and 0-3000 years at the enlightened stage. Apparently at an enlightened stage we are given some choice—for the Few, there are no set rules.

Reenter the mystics, prophets and messiahs.
From the mundane point of view, there is one thing that sets them apart. They have the knowledge, and hence the power, to consciously manipulate what we call matter. Now that we know that (according to our science) all matter is energy at different rates of vibration, and that our reality is an illusion, this ability sounds a lot easier to accept.

All we need do, here and now, is to imagine what our "heaven" should be like, and act as though we could bring it about. We know that "like attracts like", no matter how illusory. In fact, the Universal Laws seem to indicate that similar rates of vibrations attract and gravitate to each other. If you believe in happiness, the chances are much greater that you will be happy. The same goes for all other traits of character which, being states of consciousness, are the only energy that is real. Yes, even here, on Earth. In fact:

CONSCIOUSNESS
is the only
Creative Energy in the Universe.

All else is elusive, transient, unreal as is all of reality detectable by our human senses. We were, are, and will be individualizations of the Omnipresent Creative Energy of Consciousness, until we choose to give up our individuality, *i.e.*, our Ego, and decide to blend, once again, with the

Omnipresent Consciousness.

> *"He that overcomes...*
> *he shall go out from there no more..."*
> (Revelation 3:12 KJV)

The ancient scribes suspected this truth, but didn't have our modern idiom to express it.

So, once again, all we really must do, here, on Earth, in this illusory reality, is to make sure that our likes and dislikes are such as would assure us of happiness for say... 1,500 years. We must always remember that time is a dimension of phenomenal realities. Our state of Being remains in the eternal Now. Our Becoming is subject to Universal Laws controlling a particular phenomenal reality. It all has to do with the rates of vibrations of energy.

Thus, *Devachan* is evidently an extended, though still transient phenomenal reality, though, I strongly suspect, at a higher rate of vibrations.

Of course, we have no idea what Universal Laws might govern other beings, other individualizations of Omnipresent Consciousness, on other planets throughout the phenomenal Universe. Yet I strongly suspect that the Laws are the same for all realities controlled by similar or identical rates of vibrations of energy. The rates might increase as the Universe expands towards infinity.

However, since we are 'Earthlings' of, as yet, very limited intellectual capacity, I shall limit myself to the "here and now". (PS. I, too, am an Earthling!)

Later, in another stint on Earth, we might change our minds and reach even higher realities.

I also strongly suspect that Devachan is merely another state of consciousness, in which we create a reality that suits our predilections, at least for an extended while.

But whatever happens, whatever the truth about building our realities, of one thing I am certain. There is no *"requiescat in pace"*. And if there were such a condition, it would be my version of Hell. Imagine spending 1500 years of undisturbed peace without any challenges to conquer.

Not for me.

Hence, to repeat Theodore Roosevelt, *"Do what you can, with what you have, where you are."*

I'd add, whenever you are.

~~~

(1) Mahatma means "great soul", derived from Sanskrit (*maha*) meaning "great" and (*atman*) meaning "soul, spirit, life".

(2) 2 Corinthians 12:2

(3) Luke 17:21 et alii.

(4) Mark 8:27 et alii

(5) Matthew 16:13–16; Mark 8:27–29; Luke 9:18–20

Chapter 3
HERMAPHRODITES
(What We Were)

> *"The results of political changes are hardly ever those which their friends hope or their foes fear."*
> **Thomas Huxley, (1825 - 1895)**
> British biologist

> *"Love is the longing for the half of ourselves we have lost."*
> **Milan Kundera (1929 -)**
> Czech Author

> *"Our ancestor was an animal which breathed water, had a swim-bladder, a great swimming tail, an imperfect skull & undoubtedly was an hermaphrodite! Here is a pleasant genealogy for mankind."*
> **Charles Darwin (1809 - 1882)**
> FRS FRGS FLS FZS

Originally, we were stardust. We, the people. The human species. Yet before us, before the stars exploded to seed the ever-expanding space with its phenomenal, ever more complex ingredients, there had been other gods, other intelligent species, who created the stars. By now those magnificent creators may have merged again with the Omnipresent Consciousness, enriching Its inexhaustible creative potential with the complexity they contributed to the phenomenal reality of the primordial past. Hence the Creative Energies grew exponentially, ever faster, ever greater, until the Phenomenal Universe became almost real.

Or so it seemed, and so it continues to appear to us.

To us, the children of Eden, who by Universal standards

only recently became aware of our divine heritage. We, the human species, for the most part still think that the phenomenal Universe, the phenomenal reality, is real.

Alas, it is all an illusion.

The whole Universe is but an expression of our and our predecessors' consciousness. Of our artificial intelligence created not so long ago.

No, not through a Big or Little Bang. That was but a local occurrence. Our origin lies in the individualization of the Omnipresent Creative Energy of Consciousness. Even as everyone of the more than 37 trillion cells in each of our bodies knows its place, knows its function, so, eventually, we, each one of us, will become aware of our place, our function in the phenomenal Universe.

No matter how transient the illusion, the joy of creation will be ours.

After all, even our presence, here, on earth, is not real. Only our Consciousness is. When it leaves us, when it leaves our bodies, we, the real we, will be here... no more. Our true Consciousness is indestructible. It will last forever, while our artificial intelligence, our Ego, will metamorphose into countless other energies of different vibrations, until it merges with its Source.

On the other hand our Egos might not survive. For most of us, our egos are part of the transient phenomenal reality, hence serving the sole purpose of survival in the phenomenal reality. Thus, it is not immortal. Only those serving the enrichment of the phenomenal reality, of contributing to the complexity and enhancement of the Universe will last forever. Or, as mentioned above, until they choose to merge with their Origin; choose to be reabsorbed into the endless ocean of Omnipresent Consciousness.

Other egos, like all energies of lower vibrations are subject to renewing. Their energies may be recycled in the hearts of a Black Holes to their original rate of vibration, and start again on the evolutionary trek towards the fulfillment of their function. To the glorious destiny of contributing their creative effort towards enhancing and adding diversity to the phenomenal Universe.

Eventually we shall not need the artificial intelligence of the Ego. And, once we shed it, we shall become aware of the omnipresent Oneness.

Oneness of time and space.

Of the intangible reality.

We shall blend with the Omnipresent Consciousness which the vast majority of people call God.

More about this in the final chapter.

Coming back to Eden. To Paradise. To the reality we might have never left if it hadn't been for the 'apple'. For the temptation of knowledge. Yes, as individualizations of the Omnipresent Consciousness we couldn't resist the temptation to gain knowledge that would help us to contribute to the phenomenal reality. *"Lead us not into temptation,"* comes to mind. We needed to create. To be... gods, before we learned the Universal Laws.

Yet, we needed to enhance the Universe.

To leave our mark.

To add to the creative diversity.

Instead, in spite of all the good intentions, we succumbed to the sin of pride.

Indeed... long before we became hermaphrodites, we were pure, intangible individualizations of Consciousness, gallivanting among the luscious splendor of primeval nature created by our predecessors, looking for a suitable phenomenal body to invade and make our own.

But even then we were running billions of years ahead of ourselves. We had to gather experience of what the phenomenal life is about. It all began with:

> *"The earliest known life-forms on Earth are putative fossilized microorganisms, found in hydrothermal vent precipitates, that may have lived as early as 4.28 billion years ago, relatively soon after the oceans formed 4.41 billion years ago, and not long after the formation of the Earth 4.54 billion years ago."*
>
> (Abiogenesis in Wikipedia)

Are you sure you want to go that far back? Someone did. Someone did and guided the earthly evolution by adding complexity to the original microorganisms. Everything and everyone must have a cause and effect, and evolution advances through enhancement and complexity. The same is true, to this day, of the whole Universe.

As for us, simple folks, over seven octillion years (that's 7 billion-billion-billion) ago, those mindless invisibly small particles we know as atoms congealed to make a human form. Each atom has been directed to its rightful place, and performs the function to which it has been and continues to be assigned. According to atheists, it all happened by accident, and... according to our scientists, the atoms appeared out of nothing.

Remember Big Bang?

All of them, billions and billions and billions of them found their place. Are you sure they are mindless?

It must feel silly being an atheist. Or... fundamentalist scientist for that matter. Or any fundamentalist.

I still think that Socrates was right.

We don't know much...

Nevertheless, in spite of our friendly atheists, those mindless atoms combined to form some 37.2 trillion cells. Countless different cells with different duties to perform.

And then in every cell there appeared strands of DNA whose sole job was, and is, to reproduce themselves.

(The set of chromosomes in a cell makes up its genome; the human genome has approximately 3 billion base pairs of DNA arranged into 46 chromosomes.)

(Wikipedia)

And they do it with such efficiency that the information they store becomes immortal. Hence our heritage dates back to fish and all sorts of hairy cousins, which to this day enjoy their inimitable characteristics. And if we are very, very smart, we can actually reach back to our primordial history in our dreams. We can fly and swim like birds and fish. Isn't DNA smart?

Are you sure all this happened by accident?

Or does some strange, infinite, intelligent energy of Omnipresent Consciousness have something to do with it?

Omnipresent.

It 'tells' every single cell what to do. And every atom. And every subatomic particle. On the other hand, isn't all energy? Perhaps it is the energy that carries intelligence. Omnipresent Energy? Didn't they call it Spirit once? Aren't we all just manifestations of this Energy?

Except for the atheists, of course.

You decide.

Yet not all ingredients of our bodies are as immortal. Our hair and skin attest to that. Don't worry if your hair is falling out. With luck, it should stick on your head for up to seven years. But its roots stay behind and continue to grow. Unless you are old and gray, of course. Then you need a bit of luck.

Your skin, the outside layer of skin called epidermis,, is quite another story. As we walk around, every hour we shed...

> *"...around 1.5 million dead skin flakes. We recognize them as dust on our floors. But not to worry. A veritable army of insatiable mites spends their entire existence eating up bits and pieces of our dead, dried-up pieces of skin. Epidermal delight."*
>
> *Beyond Religion I*
> ("An Inquiry into the Nature of Being")

And DNA provides us with more evidence for the unity of the Universe, for the Oneness I allow myself to insist on:

> *"All humans share 99.9% of their DNA, yet no two humans are alike. My DNA and your DNA will differ in three to four million places, which is a small proportion of the total but enough to make a lot of difference between us."*[1]

And now, having begun some 4.28 billion years ago, let us jump forward by a billion years. We must remember that in the non-phenomenal reality time does not exist. In a manner quite incomprehensible to our artificial intelligence, everything happens in the eternal NOW. In fact, it already exists in its potential form, waiting to become manifest in the phenomenal reality.

So by 'now', if we are to believe our scientists, there are some 100 trillion microorganisms living happily in a human body, although I have serious doubts how many scientists have actually counted them. Regardless of their mathematical accuracy, that's a lot more than the 37.2 trillion cells of our body. And yet... and yet each human cell knows exactly its nature, its function, its place in the scheme of things.

Omnipresent Intelligence? Consciousness?

You decide.

By contrast, we, motivated by the consciousness generated by our brain, by the 100 billion neurons (a mere fractions of other cells making up our bodies), often have problems coordinating the behaviour pattern of three or four members of our family.

There is, however, a consolation.

While each individual cell or microorganism has very limited lifespan, we, the 'total' we, the 'real' Consciousness residing within this magnificent engineering achievement, which took billions of years to construct — *we are immortal.*

Perhaps this is the place to mention what I mean by the 'real' we. From the Mosaic ancient history, real "I am" was, and remains to be referred to as our "Higher Self". When asked how he obtained the inspiration that generated the Ten Commandments, intended to enhance and enrich our life on Earth, Moses replied:

*"The one who **IS** called **I AM has sent** me to **you**."*

Notice the present tense. I AM exists beyond time.

This phrase illustrates that this knowledge regarding our reality has been known in ancient times. It illustrates the transfer of knowledge from the Higher Self to the Ego.

Since that time, however, it is evident that the human ego grew at the expense of the ancient wisdom. Furthermore, it should be noted that while our ego is subject to virtually constant metamorphosis, our Higher Self *is*, and thus has been immortal from the instant of Its individualization.

There are consequences.

While the majority of us rely on technology to eliminate the need for creative thinking from our biological lives, a few, the Chosen Few, continue to enhance and improve the vehicles, which enable us to enhance and improve the diversity of the Universe. To repeat, that's our job:

To enhance and improve the Universe.
By adding beauty and diversity.

Back to our phenomenal bodies. Regardless of the immortality of our true Self, we mustn't worry about our cells. Although each individual cell's life lasts from a mere few hours to, sometimes, a few days, they reproduce themselves by dividing to create new cells (*mitosis*)[2]. They make a copy of all their chromosomes (which are coiled strands of DNA), thus extending the existence of the genetic material that holds the instructions for all life. This reproductive process of producing identical copies lasts for as long as we remain within their structures. (As long as our bodies manifest life, *i.e.*, biological functions.)

Many of the 100 trillion bacteria fall into this same category, particularly those that need a host to survive. We are the hosts, of course. Regrettably, the same applies to cells carrying diseases from plants or animals.

So, that's what we were.
In fact, still are.
Milking cows for trillions of microorganisms.

Oh, all right. That's what our bodies are. Are we more than that? Are you?

Luckily, evolution in her inspired wisdom (the Omnipresent Consciousness?) developed our immune system which, while still not well understood, offers us the first line of defence from foreign microorganisms.

And now, perhaps none too soon, we can discuss the human form. Originally, we were all hermaphrodites. Before the Creative Energy (God) "created" Eve, remember? Then, in order to enhance our reproductive system, 'nature' (again, the Creative Energy or the Omnipresent Consciousness) decided that we were sufficiently evolved to split our reproductive system. After innumerable millennia, this evolutionary step took place when the enormity of the memory stored in the (human hermaphroditic brain) needed a greater storage capacity (additional neurons if not a whole neurological system). The subconscious, as indeed all forms of Consciousness other than that generated by our brain, are not a "physical" phenomenal energy, but aspects of it necessary for human survival are stored in our neurological system.

Apparently, the subconscious inspires our emotions, while the conscious mind is required for non-physical creative endeavours, such a music, poetry and other forms of art. The good news is that all forms of art spring from the successful interplay of the lower (Ego) and Higher Self.

In the artistic endeavours, we participate in the enhancement of the Universe. Any form of 'art' that does not fulfill this function, simply is NOT art. It is no more than an expression of our flamboyant egos.

Yet there is another reason for the termination of hermaphroditism in our ancestors, and it is neither physical nor metaphysical. It is the need of diversity. Physically a hermaphrodite is defined as:

> *"...an organism that has complete or partial reproductive organs and produces gametes normally associated with both male and female sexes."*
>
> (Hermaphrodite, Wikipedia)

Yet there is more, much more to this characteristic. As Siddhartha Mukherjee wrote in *The Gene: An Intimate*

History (Scribner; Reprint edition), "humans don't actually reproduce at all. Geckos reproduce; we recombine."

Cloning continually passes on all its genes to the next generation. It protects the integrity of the species, but also makes it susceptible to pathogens.

With conventional sex, each partner passes only half of his and her genes to their progeny. The second generation does likewise. By the time your great-great-grandchildren are born, they inherit only one-sixteenth of the original genes from each of their great-great-gramdparents.

This not only satisfies the Universal need for diversity, but it also protects the species from external pathogens. In addition, while it may be responsible for the diminution of the talents of some of their grandparents the individuals are more likely to produce a Leonardo da Vinci, an Albert Einstein, a Shakespeare or a Verdi.

And... regrettably, multifarious members of the "Third Party" (discussed in Chapter 8).

Diversity is thus a *sine qua non* for Universal expansion.

To summarize *"what* **we were"** is equally as enigmatic a concept as to accept *where* we are at present. Assuming that we accept the concept of evolution, we, our artificial intelligence, must have evolved from some lower states of consciousness, irrespective of what phenomenal bodies they occupied. We tend to underestimate the intelligence and inherent knowledge of many species which preceded ours. This, however, is not as simple as it sounds.

The problem, as always, was created equally by our religious and scientific fraternities. Only the Buddhists accept that the Universe was never created but that it continues to recreate itself eternally. On the other hand, Buddhism is not really a religion. It is a way of life as, though not many will agree, Christianity had been intended to be. That was before St. Paul decided that bird in hand is better than a flock in the sky. Contrary to Yeshûa's assurances that Heaven is **within** us, St. Paul disagreed.

> *St. Paul's kingdom*
> *was firmly established on Earth,*
> *in an illusory reality of the*
> *phenomenal Universe.*

Unfortunately, and incredible though it may sound, all Paul's successors continued, and continue to this day, to ignore the teaching of Yeshûa, of the man they affirm to be their Master if not God. Yet, all of leaders of Christendom proclaim to be his followers, while grasping the elusive bird by its tail.

*They studiously ignore the affirmation **"Ye are gods"** and prefer to affirm **"Ye are sinners"**.*

Likewise, Yeshûa's affirmation that ***"Heaven is within you"**,* fell of deaf ears.

[By the way, you might care to read my novel *PETER & PAUL*, to see that Paul had big problems with the essence of Yeshûa's teaching, in addition to his preoccupation with the phenomenal reality. After all, some 2000 years later, our late pope Ioannes Paulus II, (known in Polish as Jan Paweł II), who was since raised to the status of a saint, had been a self-confessed phenomenalist.] [3]

And who can blame them?

The Jewish Torah asserts that the world was created on October 7th, 3761 BCE. The Christians obediently followed the Hebrews pushing the date only slightly back. James Ussher (1581-1656), the famous and respected Archbishop of Ireland assured us that, in fact, it took place on October 23, 4004 BCE.

The scientists, not to be outdone, proudly proclaimed

that the world started from the Big Bang some ***13.8 billion years ago,*** although:

> *...life could have begun as early as 17 million years after the Big Bang...*
>
> (Wikipedia, Abiogenesis)

Later, the "short gap" between 17 million and 13.8 billion years seems to have stretched to quite a few billion years. Elsewhere, the very same Wikipedia asserts that the earliest known life forms on Earth (putative fossilized microorganisms) first appeared at least 3.77 billion years ago (although it may have been as early as 4.28, or even 4.5 billion years ago.) [4]

No matter. What's a few billion years between friends? And, after all, no one expects scientists to be good at mathematics. To quote Einstein:

> *"Do not worry about your difficulties in Mathematics. I can assure you mine are still greater."*

However, while the Jewish and Christian "Heaven and Earth" had been created by God, the scientists' Universe appeared out of thin air, although even air wasn't around at the time. It just happened out of nothing. It seems to me that too many scientists concentrate too much on nothing.

I'd rather be a Jew or a Christian and have a progenitor, no matter how unlikely. After all, why would a God create a world knowing what a mess we were going to make out of it? Surely, an all-knowing God would have known better.

The only aspect they (religionists and scientists) all agree on is that there is but one world. While Christians accept that there are many Heavens,[5] they insist on placing them outside of the phenomenal realities. In a way, they are right, although I'd suggest that they can coexist. (I'd also suggest they confuse them with *Devachans*).

We now know that none of the *Devachans* are real, either. Or at least no more real than the realities in which, at present, we all enjoy our becoming.

And yet, after all this rigmarole of absurd dates, Aristotle argued that the world must have existed from eternity. (Aristotle's *Physics*)

Bingo!

But it did not happen at once, with or without a bang.

It evolved?

As the scientists deal only with the illusory image of the phenomenal Universe, they are, *perforce*, limited to the observable Universe. And such, according to them, occurred, happened, popped into existence around 13.8 billion years ago.

Exit religions.

But, as so often happened in the past, the Buddhists were right. Just recently, Stephen Hawking, the famed theoretical physicist, put an end to the beginning of the Universe. Borrowing the idea from the *string theory*, he and Thomas Hertog claimed that our Universe is eternal. That it never had a singular moment of creation.

Exit scientists?

One up for Aristotle and Buddhists.

It seems like a good time to return to the pensive question: *What were we?* Well, we were, we are, and we always shall be energy. A very complex assembly of energies vibrating at different rates, which have the power to metamorphose into various combinations of complexity.

In her book, *Miracle of Metaphysical Healing,* Evelyn Monahan, states that we are magnificent human beings, without equal in all creation.

Not quite 'gods', but still, *"without equal in all creation"*. I wonder what's happening on Andromeda. I suspect she was referring to Earth. To our tiny ball of dust. Nevertheless, you'll find in Chapter 17 that she had every right to make this statement.

And another much, much, much tinier ball of dust is our head, home to our brain. Imagine. Within this tiny ball, a three pound spongy mass, up to 80% water, with consistency of soft butter, is responsible, at least in part, for the near infinite diversity of the phenomenal universe.

Apparently, there is an mysterious reason for that.

David Eagleman, a brilliant American neuroscientist, author, and adjunct professor at Stanford University, claims that: *"in a single cubic centimeter of brain tissue there are as many synaptic connections as there are stars in the Milky Way."* Not in the whole brain but just in... a single cubic centimeter...

It seems that Evelyn Monahan was right.

We are magnificent human beings. How very few of us seem to realize it. And yet thousands of years ago, they suspected that we are gods...

Around 1991, I've seen a movie *"Defending your Life"*. Albert Brooks and Meryl Streep met in a halfway station, where the judges would decide if our heroes were to proceed to the never-never land (*Devachan*, see Chapter 2), or go back to earth for another stint of learning. The functionaries who provided the judges with evidence on which to make their decisions were very advanced human beings. They used up to 20% of the capacity of their brain.

The delinquents, perhaps, up to 4%.

Contrary to this delightful film whose conclusions are most convincing (though illusory but, after all, what isn't?) the celebrated Bill Bryson contradicts those numbers. He writes in his book, *The Body*:

> *"...the idea that we use only 10% of our brains is a myth. No one knows where the idea came from, but it has never been true or close to true. You may not*

use it all terribly sensibly, but you employ all your brain in one way or another."

Speaking for myself, I've never heard a less convincing argument in my life. While I am more than willing to accept that more than 80% of the 100 billion (lately reduced to an average of 86 billion) neurons are needed to maintain, coordinate, orchestrate, repair, and replace cells of the physical enclosure in which we live, I refuse to accept that even 20% of the residual number is used constructively for creative thinking.

Judging by the recent behaviour pattern of some politicians, I'm not convinced they use their brain at all.

(I refuse to tell you my percentage.)

As for the dimension of time, I have discussed it at length in my book "**VISUALIZATION—Creating Your Own Universe**", the chapter on *Ageing and Longevity*.[6] Forever remembering that time is a dimension of the phenomenal Universe only, you might enjoy it.

Until recently, there was an age-old struggle among the scientists (time changes with velocity) to determine if time really exists. God is eternal, all else is transient. Transiency implies time. The phenomenal reality is transient. According to Einstein, it is also illusory. That being the case time itself exists only in the phenomenal, transient, illusory reality.

Enter religions:

God is eternal, omnipresent, hence timeless. He/She/It cannot go anywhere because being omnipresent He/She/It is already there. Hence no time is required to define His/Her/Its location. It would be much easier if we stopped creating a God in our image. If we define God as an omnipresent, eternal POTENTIAL Energy, then all things would already exist in their potential form, and that would include you, and me, of the past, present and future. Hence we can exclude time from the permanent equation and limit its manifestation to just the phenomenal reality.

Voilà, problem solved.

Under these circumstances, all possible phenomenal versions of 'I', or 'you' already exist, and all we need do is to invoke them to the present, wherein we can experience his/her characteristics. To put it in more scientific jargon, all versions of me, past, present or future, already exist in the Quantum Field. At least, that's my theory. As time doesn't really exit, and all takes place in the eternal Now...

> *"In theoretical physics,* quantum *field theory is a theoretical framework that combines classical field theory, special relativity, and quantum mechanics."*
> (Wikipedia)

That's pretty much all there is, hence, all is all, no matter how complex.

With a little effort we can invoke our many facets into the present, and benefit or suffer from the nature and characteristic of such an 'I' as we invoke. We do it in our dreams. Lucid dreams bring such images into the present. Accomplishments of lucid dreams can become manifest into our phenomenal reality. Some sportsmen do it all the time.[7] After all, all's illusion. Not real?

Don't blame me, it's Einstein's idea.

This may be how 'miraculous' healing is done. We do not change reality by changing the phenomenal (hence illusory) form of expression. Instead we substitute our 'other' self 'suspended' in the eternal present of the Quantum Field.

Thus God, the All-Inclusive Potential Energy, neither was, not will be, but IS, beyond limitations of phenomenal reality. Or any other limitations which we have not as yet invented. Good luck.

~~~

(1) Bryson, Bill, *The Body* (Doubleday Canada)

(2) Mitosis is a process of nuclear **division** in eukaryotic **cells** that occurs when a parent **cell** divides to produce two identical daughter **cells**. During **cell division**, mitosis refers specifically to the separation of the duplicated genetic material carried in the nucleus. (Wikipedia)

(3) Earliest known life forms:
https://en.wikipedia.org/wiki/Earliest_known_life_forms

(4) Tymieniecka, Anna-Teresa, (1923 – 2014) was a Polish American philosopher, phenomenologist, founder and president of The World Phenomenology Institute.

(5) 2 Corinthians 12:2

(6) Kapuscinski, Stanislaw, *VISUALIZATION—Creating Your Own Universe,* (Inhousepress)

(7) *www.end-your-sleep-deprivation.com/lucid-dreaming and...*
Top athletes train extremely hard to gain the extra edge in their sport. But life is composed of two parts: wakefulness AND sleep. Lucid dreaming can help athletes train for their sport during sleep.

Chapter 4
METAMORPHOSIS
(The God Diffusion)

> *"A bad book is as much a labor to write as a good one, it comes as sincerely from the author's soul."*
> **Aldous Leonard Huxley (1894 - 1963)**
> British author
> (The above quotation is offered in case I need to apologize.)

> *"It is almost banal to say so yet it needs to be stressed continually: all is creation, all is change, all is flux, all is metamorphosis."*
> **Henry Miller (1891 - 1980)**
> American writer.

> *"Everything is in a state of metamorphosis. Thou thyself art in everlasting change and in corruption to correspond; so is the whole universe."*
> **Marcus Aurelius (121 - 180)**
> Roman Emperor and a Stoic philosopher.

> *"I metamorphosed from a violinist to bass-baritone, to architect, to writer. Is that enough?"*
> **Stanislaw Kapuscinski**
> (Author of this book and 40 others)

And so, religions have created a God in our image and likeness. This is not a new idea. Virtually all primitive groups of people created pantheons, often competing with each other for prestige and authority. Wikipedia offers no less than 25 pantheons that sprang all over the world seemingly designed to supervise man's behaviour.[1]

If the function of gods is to rule the world, then,

perhaps, the Pentagon ought to be included in this group. Each pantheon collected followers, believers, or just ignorant faithful.

Faithful to what?

To the invisible, punitive, uncompromising deities that offered us carrots and sticks as we once did to our children. Shouldn't gods be held to a higher standard? Zeus had quite a temper. As did Odin. As did a few others.

And then came Judeo-Christian philosophy. We can but wonder why people have such need to recognize the superiority of invisible 'beings' compared to their own potential. After all, various scriptures assured us that we are gods. It is stated quite unequivocally in both the Old and the New Testaments. And yet this assurance was, and continues to be, studiously ignored by the 'faithful', let alone by their priesthood. Perhaps they haven't noticed that the Bible has nothing to do with religion. It is, instead, full of wonderful advise how to be happy; how to live a full and fruitful life; and ultimately, how to reach immortality.

To make God more human, they, the Christian sacerdotal fraternity, declared Adam and his heavenly father God to be in each other's likeness. God had all the human traits. Michelangelo, the artist commissioned by Pope Julius II, dressed Him and Adam in equally human garments, and plastered them all over the ceiling in the Sistine Chapel next to each other.

Like father and son.

I'm not sure which of them is more divine.

Nevertheless, as such magnificent paintings were, and remain, accessible to the masses which the sacerdotal fraternity wanted to control, they elevated Yeshûa to the status of God, and having a convenient image of him being nailed to a wooden cross, they used that image to represent their concept of God.

And this **in spite of** Yeshûa's assurance that **we are all "children of the Most High"**.

Yet, no matter how hard they tried to convert the Creative Energy into a human form, they failed.

In order to accept the reality which demands CONSCIOUSNESS to be the only source of CREATIVE ENERGY, they continued to personify this trait in a human form. Furthermore, such energy, that has to be indestructible, yet foster constant metamorphosis in order to increase the DIVERSITY of the phenomenal Universe cannot, under any circumstances, be reduced to a single human form.

It is both, within us and outside of us. As such, we must accept that such an Energy is beyond the limitations of the phenomenal reality.

It must be
NOT OF THIS WORLD.

Not of this phenomenal, transient, illusory world. Not satisfied with the physical appearance or their divinity, various religions have introduced the concept of God being 'good', without ever defining what is meant by this adjective. Good for whom... for you or for me? Good for a particular species, for flora or for fauna... Does their God have any favorites, preferences?

We, and not just the priesthood, continue to assign human traits to our concept of God. Professional sportsmen invariably make a sign of the cross when entering an arena of battle, the sporting stadium. As if God kept close attention to the inerrant gladiators. Inerrant like the Bible. Like other scriptures of dozens of religions. And this in spite of the fact that the scriptures had been written by extremely errant scribes translating the original document into countless languages. Some years ago I discovered that some 3,200 words in the King James Version of the Bible have not been translated from ancient Hebrew or ancient Greek.

I was amazed.

Apparently, during the last 2,000 years, no one had noticed this glaring omission. I am an architect. If I were to make such mistakes in the design of my buildings, they would collapse. And now, I wondered, for how long can Christianity last—a religion that is based on half-truth, all the while pretending that they are following the explicit word of God.

Again, I was amazed!

I've spent the subsequent eight months in the Library of the School of Religious Studies affiliated to the McGill University in Montreal. Day after day I pored over dozens of large volumes to discover the truth.

To my further amazement, I discovered that the translations existed, but they had been omitted from the final texts.

Then I realized why. The ancient words had different meanings given them by different translators. Rather than agreeing to the best possible meaning, the 'experts', probably the PhDs of theology, or divinity, decided to keep the general public, the sheep that followed their dictates, in the dark.

And even that was not all...

A still deeper immersion into the thick volumes in the library led me to learn that various words had a very different symbolic meaning than we have now. In nearly 2000 years, the original symbolic meanings have been completely ignored.

Well, I refused to accept such blatant subterfuge.

Eight months later on June 11th, 2011, my *Dictionary of Biblical Symbolism* was published. It is still available on Amazon and other outlets. Enjoy!

Now, let us return to human divinities.

There is no such thing, or being, as God contained

within a human form. Nor could there be. If there were, it would be in constant state of contradiction, making absolutes impossible. It couldn't be infinitely just and infinitely forgiving at the same time. These are *human* traits, though certainly not infinite.

The biblical expression *"Ye are gods"* refers to our ability to metamorphose various rates of energy into other forms, and slow them down to make them perceptible to human senses. In fact to recognize some of them as material forms. Hence came the metaphysical healing that Yeshûa and dozens of other mystics since have demonstrated.

But do we practice our 'divine' attributes?

Do we believe the prophets or Yeshûa?

Most certainly not. There is much too much money in the medical and pharmaceutical industries to even attempt what in more recent years Evelyn Monahan has demonstrated as possible. More about her in Chapter 17.

Please, let us put to bed all divinities our religionists want to create in our image and likeness. No matter how magnificent such a being would be, neither It nor He, nor She, would be able to manifest in our reality.

Why?

Even the most ardent religionists agree that God is immortal. And here, on Earth, everything is not only transient but illusory. Surely, they don't want their God to be an illusion? I'll leave such arguments to theologians and advance the only solution that makes sense to me.

While "God" defined by any definition might limit *Its* nature, It does appear to manifest the following characteristics:

INFINITE OMNIPRESENT INEXHAUSTIBLE ENERGY OF CONSCIOUSNESS

Why specifically Consciousness? Because it is the only

energy that vibrates at an *infinite rate*, and hence is *omnipresent* and *all-inclusive*.

Furthermore, such energy must have the ability to metamorphose into infinite diversity of rates of vibrations, thus manifesting in an infinite number of forms.

"God Diffusion" mentioned in *DELUSIONS* is little more than *spontaneous metamorphosis*. The spontaneity is due to the creative nature of the energy, let alone of the Omnipresent Consciousness. Few of us seem to be aware that this metamorphosis is an ongoing process which, thanks to the diversity supplied by the artificial intelligence generated by our brains, is responsible for the *continuous expansion of the phenomenal Universe*.

Only the infinite rate of vibrations is indestructible. The slower rates of energy are transient, but they can be metamorphosed into other rates that exhibit other characteristics.

It seems that not only in a Kindergarten children need the authority of parents or teachers to guide them. At our evolutionary stage, however, our adults extended this proclivity to the grown ups. Perhaps we all need an authority that would guide us in our lives. At least, until we *really* grow up? Not physically but in our consciousness. Yes, in our artificial consciousness. The consciousness that adds to the diversity of creation within our phenomenal Universe.

In this sense, we really are gods. Or can be...

On the other hand, we, the real we, are immortal. Perhaps in a million years or so, we shall learn to stand on our own feet.

Until then we, or most of us, suffer most from the disciplines which various religious sects impose on us.

Freedom of religion, so praised by the people at large, allowed the imported and indigenous religions to flourish in great diversity. As the majority of Americans declared themselves to be of Christian persuasion, I shall limit myself to comments about Judeo-Christian ethics.

In the USA, as of 2019, 65% (down from 73.7 two years earlier) of the populations confessed to being Christians. I've read that world-wide, there might be as many as 33,000 Christian denominations. It's a good place to start.

As a matter of fact, diversity is to be praised rather than condemned. After all, the expansion of the Universe is due principally to the expansion of the ideas that swell our consciousness. This may be our unwitting yet positive contribution to the Universe.

So, as you can see, while Ego has its negative traits, it is also indispensible to the survival of its phenomenal hosts, as well as for the experimentation with new ideas flowing from our unconscious.

All ideas originate in our UNCONSCIOUS.

As mentioned, such new ideas which find a foothold in the phenomenal Universe assure continued growth of Universal Diversity.

To assure constant growth, the Universe produces new species. Periodically, various species which exhausted its phenomenal potential are allowed to become extinct, making room, within the same environment, for new diversity.

There is neither love nor hate involved in this. We must never forget that our world is *not real*. No more so than the realities we experience in our dreams. And ALL phenomenal energies, while indestructible, are subject to metamorphosis.

And now, to put the whole problem of a 'religious' God or gods away, allow me to quote what has been known to us for more than two thousand years:

The kingdom of God is within you.

Not in the corpse after you 'die', nor even in some other phenomenal reality but *within you*. Here and now.

>Kingdom of God is:
>**A STATE OF CONSCIOUSNESS.**
>All you need do is to find it.
>Again, *here and now*.
>And let me assure you, if you don't find it here and now, then, sooner or later, you'll start looking for it again and again until you do. That's what reincarnation is all about. So... keep looking and, please, don't give up. It is waiting for you.

~~~

(1) 25 Pantheons:
African, Armenian, Aztec, Buddhist, Berber, Canaanite, Celtic, Chinese, Egyptian, Germanic, Greek, Guanche, Hindu, Incan, Jain, Japanese, Japanese Buddhist, Maya, Native American, Norse, Rigvedic, Roman, Slavic, Sumerian, Yoruba... and many other pantheons. Some pantheons had a number of variants.

Chapter 5
MANY ARE CALLED
(The Beginning and the End)

> *"Pragmatism asks its usual question. 'Grant an idea or belief to be true,' it says, what concrete difference will its being true make in anyone's actual life? How will the truth be realized?"*
> **William James, (1842 - 1910)**
> American psychologist and philosopher

> *"Many are called but Few are Chosen."*
> **Matthew 22:14 KJV**

> *"I am just a child who has never grown up. I still keep asking these 'how' and 'why' questions. Occasionally, I find an answer."*
> **Stephen Hawking (1942 - 2018)**
> English theoretical physicist, cosmologist

As already mentioned in various contexts, the 'Beginning' ends when we start listening to the silent voice within. Quite "many are called"[1] and they begin to suspect that there is more than just the phenomenal Universe. That energies are not only those defined as such by our aspiring scientists, but that they include all forces that contribute to the reality we live in. Even the forces, or energies, that cannot be measured by the most sophisticated technological instrumentation.

Nevertheless, quite a few are *called*.

At this stage the 'call' is a whisper vaguely perceived, of course, by our artificial consciousness. By our Ego. By the consciousness generated by our phenomenal, hence illusory brain. Our true Self, the *I AM*, is the sender of the call.

But, it's a start. A blessed, wondrous start.

It is the period of transition.

Also, this is the only part of the phenomenal stage of our evolution that is controlled by our artificial intelligence. We might call it the Kindergarten in which we are gradually becoming aware of who we are. Of who we *really* are.

It is indeed the Beginning of the End of the illusory existence. Of the transient illusion.

It is the first step towards finding our way back to Eden. To Paradise. Remember, the Paradise is within you. Within every one of us. And from within come the inspirations of the great artists. Perhaps the most famous example of creativity coming from within is given us by Ludwig von Beethoven (1770 - 1827). He is reported to have dated his hearing loss from buzzing noises he suffered in 1798.

> *"For two years I have avoided almost all social gatherings because it is impossible for me to say to people 'I am deaf',"* he wrote. *"If I belonged to any other profession it would be easier, but in my profession it is a frightful state."*

Other sources date the start of his losing hearing from the age of 26. By the time he reached 44, he was almost totally deaf. It must have been devastating for him. Yet he composed his 3rd symphony, the *Eroica*, when he was already 33 well on the way of becoming deaf.

A prominent reviewer proclaimed the *'Eroica'*, which Beethoven composed in 1803 (and premiered in Vienna in 1805), as *"one of the most original, most sublime, and most profound products that the entire genre of music has ever exhibited."*

"By 1824, at the end of the premiere of his Ninth Symphony, he had to be turned around to see the tumultuous applause of the audience because he could hear neither it nor the orchestra."

(Wikipedia)

His heavenly music must have come from a heavenly source, from Heaven that he discovered within himself.

There are many other examples of great ideas that were born "within", that originated in our dreams, in fact in *lucid-dreams*.

Einstein's speed of light; Mary Shelly's first Sci-Fi novel; Paul McCartney's "Music that Inspires Music"; Niels Bohr's structure of an atom, Elias Howe's invention of a sewing machine; the mathematical genius of Srinivasa Ramanujan who proved more than 3,000 mathematical theorems in his lifetime; and many other original thoughts and creative ideas, both scientific and artistic, have their origin in dreams.

In our unconscious.

Our creative source is inexhaustible. All we need do is find it. Within.

As mentioned in *DELUSIONS*, *Infinity has neither beginning nor end.* If it had, it would not be infinite. It cannot abide in the past, nor in the future. It can only exist in the present. It can exist only in the eternal NOW.

Heaven is beyond the limitations of time.

Or any dimension.

Or any limitation.

Heaven neither was, nor will be.

Heaven IS.

This, however, does not apply to the phenomenal reality. Thanks to Einstein, we already know that the 'reality' in which we live is not real. As already mentioned, that it is an illusion even though... *a very persistent one.*

Hence, we, a species that in terms of infinity are still in the kindergarten, regard it as real.

And... strangely enough, so we should!

The purpose of the phenomenal reality is to test if the theoretical creative potential can assume a phenomenal form. Whether the theory and practice can coexist. As stated, this theoretical potential is the reality that abides in the eternal *NOW*. Perhaps erroneously, most religions do *not* recognize a Heaven that can be experienced while still within our physical bodies. While still 'alive'. As a place where no harm can come to anyone whose consciousness has merged with the Omnipresent Creative Energy.

Well, they are wrong. Heaven is *within us*.

Nevertheless, this Consciousness of Heaven lacks the aspect of practical, no matter how transient, reality. It is like talking about love never having loved anyone. Like imagining beauty without ever having seen the incredible wonders of nature. It is like talking about the Universe, never having seen the night sky peppered with countless stars and galaxies.

Yet Heaven is none of these things.

Heaven is a condition, a state, a consciousness of infinite, inexhaustible, indestructible Potential. An infinite plethora of Energy waiting to be used. To be manifested. To be made 'real', even for just a little while. Even for a fraction of the illusory eternity. It is the Energy of irrepressible creative desire. For this Energy it is the becoming that matters. A becoming that strives ever-closer to the perfection of the Infinite Potential.

"Be ye therefore perfect, even as your Father which is in heaven is perfect," (Matthew 5:48) as Yeshûa is said to have said, in his inimitable, poetic way.

By the way, have you noticed the word 'which' rather

than 'who'? The scribes didn't manage to stray from the truth.

And this is where we come in.

We are Its means of becoming. The instruments. The carriers of life.

We are the sensual part of the creative process. However, there is a price to be paid for the experience of life. The price is the time factor. As we cannot experience infinity in a transient body, we are destined to experience only tiny fractions of the wonder of the Creative Process.

We can partake in It to the degree to which we can become aware of the wondrous Creative Energy within us. Yes, it is the same Energy that created, and continues to create, the infinity of the Universe. We are tiny, Lilliputian gods, doing our best with what we got...

And then comes the painful part. People call it death.

But *there is no death!*

Our true Self simply transfers its energy of consciousness to a reality of higher rate of vibration. If our ego deserves it, they move together. When we fulfill our *dharma*, our destiny, we give up our illusion of phenomenal life on Earth, at least for a while.

Yet our destination is also transient. Until the next chance we get to advance a minute fraction towards our true potential. Infinity always recedes beyond the next horizon.

And this applies not only to us.

Other species are also given periods of rest. Of their artificial consciousness abiding in a reality of higher rate of vibration. This is an ongoing evolutionary process.

The only difference between us and other species is the rate of vibration of the energy generated by our brain. Other species continue to abide in the Garden of Eden. They, for the most part, obey the dictates of nature (which reacts to the dictates of Higher Consciousness). If not, they die, only to be born again and keep trying. A little like us. The only yet fundamental difference is the absence of pride in their ego. Oh, yes, they also have egos, but they do not suffer from the hunger of power that only knowledge can give. Power to rule others. To dominate others. To bask in our own pride.

Have you noticed that a dog or a cat, abandoned, never blames others, their so-called masters. "What have I done wrong?" they seem to ask themselves. And if reunited, their joy is effusive. Never mixed with a sense of guilt let alone accusation.

No. Other species still enjoy subliminal obedience to the Universal Laws. Whatever they might be.

We do not.

Periodically, various species that have exhausted or fulfilled their phenomenal potential become extinct, making room, within the same environment, for new diversity. Yet, only nature, guided by the Universal Laws, has the ability to be preoccupied with maintaining such species beyond their allotted time. We must never forget that energy cannot be destroyed. This includes the energy that we refer to as life. Not physical life, of course, but the Energy of life which made the physical manifestation possible. The Energy which converted a single sperm and an ovum into an entity of billions upon billions of cells.

That, my friends, takes a lot of 'energy'.

The species seemingly extinct simply transfer their consciousness to another illusory carrier. They continue until their new brain produces sufficient self-awareness to become aware of their higher purpose.

If they have the potential to survive, they will. If not, then another chance will be given them later, in the infinity of phenomenal time. Nothing is ever wasted. Their contribution to diversity is absorbed by the Potential, to be used, again and again, to contribute to still greater diversity. Thanks to them, and us, and all the fauna and flora, the Universe continues to expand.

Yes, fauna *and flora*.

Imagine.

A tree draw water from its roots and sucks it up to feed leaves up to 300 feet high, at the very top of their branches. There, the leaves absorb carbon dioxide from the air to produce oxygen.

How?

It takes six molecules of CO_2 to produce one molecule of glucose by photosynthesis, and release six molecules of oxygen. And to create photosynthesis it draws energy from sunlight, which travels 93,000,000 miles (150,000,000 kilometers) to make this possible. The light gets here in about 8 minutes.

The oxygen keeps us alive. And not only us but all aerobic organisms. Animals and plants, even fungi and many bacteria are all aerobic and use cellular respiration to make energy. Yes, phenomenal energy that supports phenomenal life. Try not breathing for a while and see what happens to your energy.

If you think that all this can happen by accident, like the astrophysicists' big bang, than you have greater faith in accidents than I do.

Returning to 'death'.

Should any species, human or any other, make a negative contribution to the phenomenal Universe, even such would not be wasted. Energy is indestructible, but it can be metamorphosed without limits. The phenomenal locations for the recycling of such energies are the Black Holes.

Science still finds the nature of Black Holes unknown. It defines Black Holes as:

> *"...a region of spacetime exhibiting gravitational acceleration so strong that nothing—no particles or even electromagnetic radiation such as light—can escape from it. The theory of general relativity*

*predicts that a sufficiently compact mass can deform spacetime to form a **black hole**."*

(Wikipedia)
(https://en.wikipedia.org › wiki › Blackhole)

Any object exhibiting the property of mass that falls into a black hole increases its rate of vibration beyond our ability to measure it. It seems to exhibit characteristics of density. Yet, to repeat, we know that ALL IS ENERGY. It is the incredible acceleration at the end of its journey which gives the illusion of density.

And then It merges with Omnipresent Consciousness.

As for our dear scientists, they, once again, appear to have forgotten about the nature of energy. Once they remember, I'm sure they'll come up with a more logical definition.

Meanwhile, let us not forget the Event Horizon. This is the line of demarcation where the centripetal and centrifugal forces meet. These two forces maintain our reality in balance. Otherwise, the Earth would fly off into space, or crush into the sun, neither alternative propitious to our lives. Balance and growth in diversity causing constant expansion are the prerequisites of sustaining the phenomenal reality, or the Universe that (we imagine that) we know.

We can accomplish most by emulating the characteristics of the Even Horizon in our lives, in the choices we make. In relation to the enormity of the Universe, we might even call it the Straight and Narrow path of greatest success to fulfill our *dharma*. Our destiny. A state of consciousness in which we can contribute most to the diversity that will enhance the phenomenal Universe.

I know it's transient, but... it's all we've got.

Omnipresent Consciousness within us.

CONCLUSIONS

Hence, to sum up, if we abuse our powers then or there, we'll still find redemption, but at the expense of the loss of our phenomenal identity.

We shall be drawn into a Black Hole.

There, and only there, the rate of vibration of energies that failed to contribute to the Universe is accelerated to the original rate of vibrations. In fact, to the infinite rate which merges with the Omnipresent Consciousness.

This is the eternal, glorious, cycle of evolution.

~~~

(1) Matthew 22:14 KJV

Chapter 6
EDUCATION
(Why We Were)
(KINDERGARTEN)

> *"Education is what remains after one has forgotten what one has learned in school."*
> **Albert Einstein (1879 - 1955)**
> Nobel Prize in Physics in 1921

> *"Education: A succession of eye-openers each involving the repudiation of some previously held belief."*
> **George Bernard Shaw (1856 - 1950)**
> British dramatist, critic, writer.

> *"Education is an admirable thing, but it is well to remember from time to time that nothing that is worth knowing can be taught."*
> **Oscar Wilde (1854 - 1900)**
> Irish poet and playwright.

To repeat dear old Albert: ALL IS ENERGY. And various energies have a characteristic of what seems to be a magnetic attraction. Like attracts like. Similar energies, energies of similar rate of vibrations, attract each other. They blend and merge. Become one.

Imagine.

The omnipresent, perfect, immortal, indestructible Consciousness shares its attributes with us. With you and me. And a few billion others. And yet, only a *Few* of us choose to accept this magnificent gift. We prefer to rely on our Egos, the artificial intelligence generated by our biological computer. By our brain.

Amazing!

Lack of gratitude? Or just plain ignorance?

And yet this is why we are here. For millions and millions of years. Perhaps billions? Still are. We went through repeated reincarnations to begin, just begin, being aware of the munificent generosity of the Universe.

On the other hand, we've only just begun exploring our potential. Our infinite potential. We are all children of the "Most High". Of an Energy that gives us creative energy of gods.

Let us never forget that we are here to learn.

THE KINDERGARTEN

*[The essay originally printed in DELUSIONS does not raise any questions, but rather provides Conclusions. I brought the excerpts from **Beyond Religion 1, Essay #52** up to the latest knowledge available.]*

"It begins when the rudimentary consciousness asserts its will to survive as an individual unit in the phenomenal reality.

An amoeba, a virus, a bacterium.

A mono-cellular entity becomes aware of the reality within and the immediate environment outside of itself. It defines its territory, its boundaries. The primitive consciousness learns the laws of survival by re-embodying itself within ever more complex physical forms. Each re-embodiment is designed to increase the scope of its operations. The Sanskrit scriptures place the number of transmigrations of each individual consciousness at 8,400,000. Hopefully this number includes the second phase of our (human) evolution, though I doubt it. Suffice it to say that the primary stage of our existence consists exclusively of assuring physical survival and wellbeing in the phenomenal reality (through which individualized Consciousness can experience the process of Becoming).

The learning process in this phase relies on repetitive conditioning. The method is that of trial and error. The repetitions serve to develop a subconscious storehouse of information, on which the primitive consciousness can draw to survive within its embodiment in ever changing environments. Its responses to challenges are reactive, *i.e.,* automatic or instinctive.

There is no evidence of free will or deductive reasoning, although the acquired experiences are carefully stored in the genetic code of the biological constructs, and the entity proceeds to advance its evolution. At this stage, the individualized consciousness is subject to the indomitable laws of nature.

A mistake costs it its creation and its life.

Nature is a very cruel mistress.

The main problem in kindergarten is that there is no discernible communication. What little there might be, by observation only, is immediately adapted to one's own survival. Otherwise, it is ignored. This acute, purposeful self-centeredness seems to persist in some individualized unit of awareness for many eons. I know people who behave in this fashion even today, a few million years since its original embodiment.

The hypothetical phenomenon of the hundredth monkey effect comes much later. In 'School'.

Nevertheless, nature in her wisdom, has equipped our rudimentary units of intelligence with genetic memory storage, well ahead of any computer. This code carries most if not all the instructions for survival, short of the unit coming across new, unprecedented hurdles.

In such circumstances, one of two things can happen.

Either it follows the input from its genetic code, or, by accident (though not by design), it tries something new. If the new works, it becomes incorporated into the revised, enhanced code and is passed on to future generations in order to assist them in survival. I believe this is one way of looking at Darwin's "survival of the fittest," although "survival of the most resourceful" again, by accident, might be a better way to describe the kindergarten.

Nevertheless, the kindergarten is the only phase of our evolution wherein the process of natural selection reigns supreme. Millions of years of natural selection results in a veritable plethora of most diverse, complex and beautiful organisms imaginable—not the least of which is man. Alas, at the end of the school year, man and natural selection must part company.

Thus, the learned biologists must resign themselves to deal only with primitive life forms, unless they prefer to sit back, wait, and see what happens to their own bodies. It might prove to be a very, very long wait.

Energy cannot be destroyed, remember?

And, after all, *we are all... energy.*

The immortal aspect is, of course, the Energy of Consciousness, no matter in how primitive phenomenal body it finds its transient abode.

While the process of natural selection is, by definition, a process, *i.e.,* it is not limited by time and thus it continues even today in more advanced forms, *e.g.,* in humans. All too often its built-in rare but necessary tendency toward mutation, turns against the organism it helped develop, by attacking the organism's immune system. The extremely prevalent rheumatoid arthritis is a well-known example of this. I suppose one could say that if it doesn't kill one, it makes one stronger. Regrettably, it takes a lot of joy out of life.

Amusing though it may seem, there are people, today, who appear to be motivated exclusively by the above method. They have not, as yet, taken charge of their own natural selection. They still have a 50/50 chance of survival. A little like tossing a coin. In fact, I have met very few people who were willing to take full responsibility for their actions. There was always someone else to blame. Perhaps, at their stage of development, they were doing the right thing.

There is one other vital lesson that we are intended to learned in kindergarten. The lesson deals with evolutionary absolutism. It is also very pragmatic. It states quite simply: kill or be killed. You must kill to eat, thus to survive: carnivore and herbivore alike. Let us never forget that it is the same life-force that enlivens both fauna and flora. Kill or be killed is not a suggestion, it is an absolute prerequisite of natural selection.

It is unfortunate that the majority of the human species still conforms to this primitive evolutionary demand. In fact, many of us don't just kill to survive, we kill because we enjoy killing. We enjoy the hunt. It seems that natural selection has not succeeded in eliminating this trait, as yet, from the human species. Will it ever?

It will. Those (energies) which do not evolve will be recycled in the Black Holes.

Chapter 7
CAUSE & EFFECT
(Atheist's Delusion)

> *"In all life one should comfort the afflicted, but verily, also, one should afflict the comfortable, and especially when they are comfortably, contentedly, even happily wrong."*
> **John Kenneth Galbraith (1908 - 2006)**
> Canadian-American economist and author

> *"We can never obtain peace in the outer world until we make peace with ourselves."*
> **Dalai Lama**
> The 14th Dalai Lama

> *"Peace cannot be kept by force; it can only be achieved by understanding."*
> **Albert Einstein (1879 - 1955)**
> Nobel Prize in Physics in 1921

Yet... Atheists continue to think that 'it' all happened just by accident. The renowned Big Bang that apparently happened in our vicinity some time ago (reputedly some 13.8 billion years ago), no one offers any suggestions what was there 13.9 billion years ago, or even one year earlier. And this in spite of the fact that atheists, often calling themselves scientists, like to deal with facts. Tangible facts. Indisputable facts. Not some imaginary gods.

To be quite honest, I don't blame them for disowning an old man with a gray beard adorning the Sistine Chapel as the creator of the Universe, let alone for his finger enlivening Adam. In fact, I agree with them that the Creative Energy of the Universe cannot be contained in any single being, no matter how old, powerful, magnificent, experienced or wise. Even Michelangelo couldn't create one.

Infinity is infinity. It refuses to be contained.

And yet the ancients, the Buddhists, new the basic Universal Laws:

> **Cause and effect** *is the principle of causality, establishing one event or action as the direct result of another.* **Cause and effect** *may also refer to:* **Cause and effect**, *a central concept of Buddhism; see Karma in Buddhism.*
> (Wikipedia)

And the Big Bang happened out of nothing? An effect without a cause? Only scientists know how this could have happened.

Also, I am not sure if most scientists accept the concept of infinity. Not just spatial but temporal. Or even infinite potential. After all, you can't measure it, and scientists like to measure everything. Measurement limits things, brings it down to their primitive ability to understand.

Scientist like facts they can measure with their primitive senses or with their childish instrumentation. Why childish? Because in all of the 13.8 billion years the revolution in *modern science* is said to have occurred only a few centuries ago. It began with Copernicus's heliocentric theory (1473-1543) and continued with Newton's *Principia.* That was the beginning.

We're still in kindergarten.

We, and all the scientists.

Welcome to my world!

What I find sad is that they, the atheistic scientists, do not recognize the Infinite Potential, which was, and continues to be, instrumental in the continuous creation of the ever-expanding Universe. Or that *they still think* that their Universe happened out of nothing.

And that hence, there was nothing before the Big Bang.

And that Big Bang was just a local occurrence. After all, they say, there was not even space before the Big Bang. Just nothing. Nothing at all.

Remember the song... it's "All or nothing at all..." Frank Sinatra did it justice some years ago. He was right. It must be all...

Once again, the scientists appear to forget that **all is energy**. Yet the Atheists continue to think that it all happened just by accident. I don't blame them for disowning an old man with a gray beard adorning the Sistine Chapel as the creator of the Universe, let alone for his finger enlivening Adam. In fact, I agree with them that the Creative Energy of the Universe cannot be contained in any single being, no matter how old, experienced or wise. Infinity is infinity. It refuses to be contained.

What is sad is that they do not recognize that the Energy of the Infinite Potential is instrumental in the creation of the ever-expanding Universe.

They keep forgetting that all is energy.

No. This is not a personal attack on atheists. Most adherents of most established religions would classify me as one. After all, I reject all personalized divinities. What I do not reject is the Creative Energy that individualizes Itself within all people, the Energy that is inseparable from the Omnipresent Consciousness.

The conspicuous difference is the word "***Energy***".

I'm now ready to share a secret with you. To the best of my knowledge there is one atheist whom I admire more than any other. His name was Yeshûa, who became known to the masses as Jesus Christ. He, to my knowledge, was the only man who refused to recognize any divinity other than that within his own consciousness.

To repeat, he said that:

> *"The kingdom of God is within you."*
> (Luke 17:21 KJV)

Now that is an atheist I can admire, although some 1500 years earlier this fact has been pointed out by David, a very wise man, when he said: *"Ye are gods; and all of you are children of the most High"* (Psalm 82:6 KJV).[1] Of course, the Most High 'resides' in Heaven, and Heaven, according to Yeshûa, is within you. And within me. Within all of us. Not many 'Christians' know this.

Sorry atheists, David and Yeshûa beat you to it.

There is a consequence to this concept.

Now that we know that the 'Creator' is the energy that resides within us, we can get back to the business of the phenomenal reality. In order for the Most High to reside within our Consciousness, we must have been around for quite a while. Either that, or our origin is *not of this world*.

Not of the phenomenal reality.

Hence, there must be another reality?

I rest my case, and we can get back to business.

To repeat the sentiment I expressed in ***DELUSIONS***, that some 2,400 years ago Democritus of Abdera, declared that: *"Nothing exists except atoms and empty space. All else is an opinion,"* today we beg to differ. While the majority of scientists still persist in the belief that the phenomenal Universe consists of those tiny, invisible particles, the few more advanced among them introduced the concept of point particle:

CONCLUSIONS

*A **point particle** (ideal particle or **point-like** particle, often spelled **pointlike** particle) is an idealization of particles heavily used in* physics. **Its defining feature is that it lacks spatial extension: being zero-dimensional, it does not take up space.**

(https://en.wikipedia.org › wiki › Point particle)

The physicists had no choice. After all... today we know that all is energy.

And it's all Einstein's fault. And a few other scientists'. We only imagine that we see atoms. See atoms? But aren't all things made up of atoms? Of highly... *invisible* atoms???

So... what is it that we see?

Einstein claimed that it's all an illusion. All of our 'reality'.

What do you think?

Just kidding. No one ever saw an atom.

Ever.

Not even one!

~~~

(1) *David* is described in the Hebrew *Bible* as the third *king* of the United Monarchy of Israel and Judah. My dissertation of his 23rd Psalm has been recently published. (2020)

PART TWO — PRESENT

"I am going to tell you what nature behaves like. If you will simply admit that maybe she does behave like this,
you will find her a delightful, entrancing thing.
...nobody knows how it can be like that."
Richard Phillips Feynman (1918 - 1988)
American physicist,
recipient of joint Nobel Prize in Physics in 1965.
(speaking about quantum theory)

Chapter 8
KNOWLEDGE
(Fundamentalism in Religion and Science)

> *"Science is organized common sense—where many a beautiful theory was killed by an ugly fact."*
> **Thomas Henry Huxley, (1825 - 1895)**
> British biologist, defender of Darwin's theory

> *"In nature there are neither rewards nor punishments; there are consequences."*
> **Robert Green Ingersoll (1833 - 1899)**
> American social activist, orator and agnostic

> *"Education is what remains after one has forgotten what one has learned in school."*
> *"Education is not the learning of facts, but the training of the mind to think."*
> **Albert Einstein (1879 - 955)**
> Nobel Prize in Physics in 1921

Socrates had it right. "I know that I know nothing," he confessed proudly. After all, if one takes into account one's immortality, imagine how smart we shall all be a million years from now. By comparison, today we must surely be, still, pretty much an ignorant bunch of primitives.

I know I am.

I'm learning something new every single day.

And... even more so, every single night. In my dreams.

Did you know that Albert Einstein claimed to have woken up with fresh ideas? The same, reputedly, had been true of Beethoven. And of Dali, Aristotle...

Shouldn't we all try it?

And furthermore, the only knowledge that truly matters

does not originate with the phenomenal reality. And, after all, the knowledge 'within' is infinite. Both, the theoretical potential knowledge and the manifested phenomenal reality. After all, isn't that where Heaven is? Or... the knowledge suspended in the quantum field?

No wonder Socrates confessed that he knew nothing. In terms of infinity, no matter how much we know, it is but a tiny drop in an endless ocean.

And so, to repeat, Socrates had it right. I know that I know nothing. The only knowledge that truly matters, does not deal with the phenomenal reality which is no more than the reality we are capable of perceiving. After all, our reality is transient. Illusory. Not because there is something wrong with it, only because we are, as yet, unable to see what's right. Our ability to perceive the truth, the true reality, is limited by the inadequacy of our senses. Or our technological instrumentation. Or simply our inability to understand.

Nevertheless there is no need to despair.

Since we are immortal, (by 'we' I'm referring to our Higher Consciousness,) our Egos have plenty of time to improve their individual artificial intelligence, or just to start seeing the world though the perceptions of our ultimate potential. After all, time is a dimension of the phenomenal Universe, while our true Self has it Being in a different reality.

To repeat, true knowledge deals with the potential dwelling within our individualized Consciousness. Within our *unconscious*. When we attenuate our Ego, our Self takes over. Ego is intended to serve the Universe to diversify and enhance the phenomenal realty. No matter how transient...

Our Ego, as necessary as it is to our physical survival on Earth, deals only with what is already known. It can extrapolate facts brought out from within by others, but only Self can offer expansion of our reality. Our Universe? And that is, more or less, what our scientists should be doing, instead of slogging through the quagmire of our past.

Not all scientists — but most.

After all, *"Many are called but just Few are chosen."*[1]

Very, very, very few...

And please, remember, the Bible has *nothing* to do with any religion. It just proclaims the truth derived from millennia of observation, and, perhaps, from listening to the inner voices... by the *Few*. To their unconscious? There are very, very few that excel in any profession. Or in the field of arts. Or in any field. And even amongst those who have little or no education—and yet, sometimes, they manifest exemplary wisdom...

Just a few *choose* to be chosen...

This is not "scientific" knowledge. It is not knowledge derived from observation of the *illusion* of our reality.

The reverse is true of people who escape into religion. They escape because they deny the marvels of phenomenal reality, assigning all glory for it to an invisible, up there yonder, imaginary deity. In spite of assurances by their Lord and Master, Jesus Christ, that his 'father' is in Heaven, and that Heaven is within each and every one of us, they reject this premise, preferring to apply to a still 'higher' authority. Higher than Jesus, whom they worship as their God. The expression *"Ye are gods"* falls on their deaf ears.

Likewise, Moses's postulate of a great many years ago, that *"Thou shalt have no other gods before me,"*[2] has been studiously ignored. The priesthood continued to build churches, decorate them with "graven images", paintings, sculptures, and an assembly of symbols, in lieu of the Creative Force that abides within every one of us.

They, the religionists, are the true atheists.

On the other hand, thanks to them we have inherited beautiful works of art. More about that later.

However, strangely enough, the superstitions keep both the religionists and the atheists in power. Temporal power. The threat of Hell for disobedience. The power of illusion. It gives them power to control the minds of weaker people. Of the *"Third Party"*? The minds of those who haven't as yet been called. Of... the vast majority...

In 2,000 years, nothing has changed.

Who are today's *"wolves in sheep's clothing"*?[3] The rich, the obese, the exploiters of human ignorance?

This has NOTHING to do with religion.

Just money? Power?

You decide.

After all, there are no mysteries.

"Why do ye not understand my speech?"[4] Yeshûa asked. Why couldn't they understand what he was saying? Why can't they understand his words even now, 2000 years later?

Do you? Do you understand his words?

To repeat:

This has nothing to do with religion. Any religion.

~~~

(1) Mathew 22:14
(2) Exodus 20:3-5
(3) Matthew 7:15
(4) Matthew 8:43-45, John 8:43 (KJV)

Chapter 9
THE AGE OF AQUARIUS
(Where We Are)

> *"A physician without a knowledge of Astrology has no right to call himself a physician."*
> **Hippocrates of Kos (370 BC - 460 BC)**
> Greek physician considered one of the most outstanding figures in the history of medicine.

> *"We are born at a given moment, in a given place and, like vintage years of wine, we have the qualities of the year and of the season of which we are born. Astrology does not lay claim to anything more."*
> **Carl Jung (1875 - 1961)**
> Swiss psychiatrist and psychoanalyst who founded analytical psychology

> *"The greatest mystery is not that we have been flung at random between the profusion of matter and of the stars, but that within this prison we can draw from ourselves images powerful enough to deny our nothingness."*
> **Andre Malraux, (1901 - 1976)**
> French novelist, adventurer, art historian

People with an appetite for money did to the wisdom of the Zodiac what the religions have done to the wisdom of ancient mystics. Carl Jung had it right. Astrology helps us understand why we have been born at a certain time in the evolutionary cycle.

And that is all. We are free to ignore it and remain ignorant. Or we can learn and be stupid no more.

*To forget one's purpose
is the commonest form of stupidity.*

Friedrich Nietzsche

The Age of Aquarius brings us to the present. It is time for us to come of age. To grow up. To accept responsibilities for our lives and, thus, for our thoughts. And this brings us to the crux of the matter. This is where we must all learn to stand on our own feet.

All phenomenal reality is created by the energy of our thoughts. Not our brain, which is little more than a biological computer, but by our mind, which is an integral instrument of our individualized self.

There are phases in our evolution.

In one of the first stages in noted history, we have been told to "Go forth and multiply." That was the *Age of Ram*. The first major misunderstanding. The scriptures were never about the phenomenal reality but about creativity. Creativity requires the energy of thought. We were to multiply our thoughts, not our sexual activity. We were to learn to listen to new ideas pouring from our unconscious into our consciousness. And then, we were to learn to convert them into thoughts which could manifest in our phenomenal reality.

Ignorance is almost as bad as stupidity. It can be cured but not if one is stupid.[1] The stupid ones think they already know the answers to almost everything. The ignorant ones can stop being ignorant by learning. As they increase their thoughts, they increase not only their knowledge but also their ability to add diversity to the Universe. To the phenomenal Universe. To our reality.

The stupid ones don't move. They expect to be told what to do, when to do it, and how, in a vicious circle. Yet, more often than not, when informed they refuse to obey.

But some of us have learned and gained power. Power without discipline is always dangerous. Power without love is corrupting. It can be, and often is, deadly.

Hence came the Age of Pisces.

Pisces was the Age during which we have been given ample opportunity to learn to love one another. To love our neighbours. Even our enemies. The principal teacher of the Age was Yeshûa, later known as Jesus Christ. Eventually we come to know that we are all *One*. That loving others is like loving our own Selves.

This is very necessary.

With power growing exponentially within us, the danger of its abuse intensifies. Alas, we didn't learn. Wars came. They became more and more bloody. Eventually we had World Wars. Countless millions died. We still didn't learn. In 2,000 years we haven't learned to love our neighbours let alone our enemies.

Albert Einstein affirmed that he does not know "*...with what weapons World War III will be fought, but* **World War IV will be fought with sticks and stones.**"

This is the corruption of power.

On the other hand, according to today's (Feb. 27th, 2020) TV News, the obese people in the US have passed the 40% mark of the population. It is doubtful that they could throw a stone very far, let alone wield a stick proficiently. Will obesity preclude future wars? Save humanity?

Surely, obesity—that makes it hard to get up from an armchair, which makes it painful to walk never mind run; to walk up any staircase—cannot be achieved and maintained for personal pleasure. And, after all, surely obese people know that they are significantly shortening their lives...

Are they all indulging in gluttony just to save humanity?

To save the rest of us? Are they really that kind? That unselfish? Are they among the few who know that only a small percentage of Earth is habitable for us. Most of it is water, inaccessible mountain ranges, or climatically prohibitive. There may be as many as 3.5 trillion fish living in the oceans but they have the whole depth to share. We only have the surface of Earth...

Perhaps we ought to eat more fish? And obese people take up a lot of space. So, unless you are an incurable optimist, I rather doubt that they take up eating for our sake.

Unless...

Unless they are inspired at the unconscious level to sacrifice their illusory bodies... Could it be that we are all no more than illusory instruments of a Higher Intelligence, a Higher Consciousness, that overrides our will when necessary for the good of all? For the good of the species?

After all, isn't all energy? Isn't the phenomenal world just an... albeit magnificent... illusion?

Ask Einstein.

The world now supports 7.8 billion souls, and is projected to reach 10.8 billion by the year 2100. That sounds pretty ominous. Fortunately, mother nature seems to be taking steps to protect herself and the planet from human promiscuity. According to 185 studies carried out between 1973 and 2011, and recently published in the journal of *Human Reproduction Update*, sperm count in Western nations has fallen by 50%.

When vermin eat all the available food in their immediate environment, they die, or migrate to new pastures. The same is now happening with the human species. Perhaps nature will take care of our reproductive tendencies.

Nature or... the Laws inherent in the New Age?

We have now entered the Age of Aquarius. Once the Few

had been in charge. There had been Kings and Queens. Then, the so-called democracy evolved, and power spread among the many. We call them Senators, Representatives, Members of Parliaments. The plutocrats? There are quite a few of them, and they wield power. Did they learn the lessons of the Age of Pisces?

No.

The consequences were obvious. They became corrupt, instead.

The Age of Aquarius is the next step in the evolutionary attempt to multiply the instruments of Universal expansion. This can happen only through additional diversity. The more diversity the better. Good diversity enhances the Universe. Bad? Bad diversity is recycled in the Black Holes.

Nothing gets wasted.

Now, in the Age of Aquarius, the masses (what I call the *Third Party*) will come to power. They are more ignorant and probably more stupid than the leaders of the previous Age. On the other hand, not having tasted power, as yet, they will not have been corrupted by its venomous sting. There are a great many of them. Hence, they are bound to add diversity.

We don't have much time. Each Zodiac Age is said to last only some 2,150 years. In each age we are destined, or expected (by Universal Laws?) to learn a new lesson. While the previous Age of Pisces is said to have been intended to love one another, the present Age of Aquarius is said to empower an individual to create and expand his and her own consciousness. The empowerment of an individual could be, and very likely will be, very dangerous, if the lessons of Pisces were not learned adequately.

Now, we have some two millennia to consolidate our new ability before the next Age of Zodiac will present us with new challenges.

For the cognoscenti, the next Age after the Aquarian is that of Capricorn. Prepare for the unexpected. The last Age of Capricorn ended about 24,000 years ago. It lasted, as all Ages, approximately 2,000 years. We shall enter the next such Age in about 4,000 CE. By then many of us will have reincarnated again. Perhaps more than once. Probably we shall experience the reality we are creating today.

Good luck!

In all Ages of the Zodiac we must persevere until we discover our purpose, then do the best we can to fulfill it. Let us remember that the Universal wisdom assures us to be (re)born at just the right time, in the right place. The Universe needs us to enhance and diversify the phenomenal expression of its Infinite Potential. For now we must all learn to stand on our own feet.

It is time to grow up.

When I began writing *DELUSIONS*, let alone the present *CONCLUSIONS*, I was under the impression that I am all alone in regarding the world we live in as a miracle or, at the very least, as a wondrous projection of our imagination, our dreams, or of our desire for love and beauty.

Then, to my utter amazement, I discovered the statement mentioned in my *'Introduction'*, that our reality is an illusion. And this had been announced by a Nobel Laureate, Albert Einstein, a man known for his scientific rather than philosophical background.

I couldn't believe my eyes!

"All is energy, and reality is merely an illusion."

I was no longer dreaming. It seemed that, in fact, my dreams *were* the reality. And then, much later, another surprise caught up with me. Apparently, there is a group of scientists that is warming up to the theory of, what they call, *panpsychism.*[2] This philosophy (if we can call it that) seems to harmonize with concepts implicit in both Hinduism and Buddhism.

One physicist, writes Philip Perry as recently as on 25th June 2017, stated that a ***proto-consciousness*** could replace the theory of dark matter (a sentiment I gratefully approve).[3] They suspect that the Universe may be conscious. They are close to the truth. The Universe is not conscious. We are. The Universe is CONSCIOUSNESS.

PURE UNADULTERATED ENERGY OF CONSCIOUSNESS.

While in Buddhism Consciousness is the only thing that exists, once we accept that Consciousness is Energy, this philosophy would be in harmony with Einstein's conclusions.

And there is more.

In Buddhism we are all integral part of the Godhead Brahma. My own conclusion that we are all *Individualizations of the Omnipresent Consciousness* affirms this concept.

Suddenly, perhaps belatedly, I realized that I am not alone. It was a good feeling.

And this leads us to further consequences.

Amazing though it might sound, everything that happens has its reason.[4] What acts or events Christianity might call evil, in my philosophy such acts or events might be, or have been, necessary for the evolution to proceed in harmony with Being and Becoming. The so-called 'evil' events like wars—or, more bluntly, what the Christians call "seven deadly sins"—are necessary to open our eyes to the consequences of straying from the "*Straight and Narrow,*" or, as I like to call it, the *Event Horizon.*

To repeat, there are no carrots and sticks, there are only

consequences. Our 'rewards' are self-made. After all, we are all already 'blessed' beyond measure. We are all surrounded by superabundance of miracles. And they are the results of the thoughts, emotions, and actions of those who came before us. Of the vibrations they emitted. Of people who followed the Universal Laws, or what Einstein called, the "Thoughts of God".

What's in a name?

We alone create our Heavens and Hells. Like the reality in which we are now experiencing our Becoming, they are both States of Consciousness. Perhaps, at long last, we shall catch up with the ancient knowledge we lost in the process of indulging too deeply in materialism. And now, finally, scientists are slowly rediscovering the knowledge inherent within us.

After all, aren't we gods?

~~~

(1) The term originates from Latin *stupidus*, from *stupere* "be amazed or stunned." (I hate to admit that I live in almost constant amazement at the miraculous beauty of nature.) Since the word *stupid* has grown to mean "lacking ordinary quickness and keenness of mind; dull."

(2) In philosophy of mind, *panpsychism* is the view that mind or a mind-like aspect is a fundamental and ubiquitous feature of reality.

(3) The Universe may be conscious, say prominent scientists: https://bigthink.com/philip-perry/the-universe-may-be-conscious-prominent-scientists-state

(4) See Chapter 7, CAUSE & EFFECT, above.

Chapter 10
BEING & BECOMING
(What We Are)

> *"As a rule we disbelieve all the facts and theories for which we have no use. A great many people think they are thinking when they are really rearranging their prejudices."*
> **William James, (1842 - 1910)**
> American psychologist and philosopher

> *"We are slowed down sound and light waves, a walking bundle of frequencies tuned into the cosmos. We are souls dressed up in sacred biochemical garments and our bodies are the instruments through which our souls play their music."*
> **Albert Einstein (1879 - 1955)**
> Nobel Prize in Physics in 1921

> *"The day when people die once again from a scratch of a rose thorn may not be far away."*
> **Bill Bryson OBE HonFRS (1951 -)**
> A British-American author
> (with 12 honorary doctorates!)

So what have we above? A poet speaking like a scientist, or a scientist speaking like a poet? Einstein was both. And a philosopher to boot. And, if we look deeper, a metaphysician. Among the scientists, even as among the religionists, there are the Few, the Many, and... the Third Party. Einstein was definitely among the Few.

Since we all embody the creative forces of the Universe,

we are what we believe we are. Some inferior *"bundles of frequencies"* (formulating artificial intelligence) think they are clever, and, in their eyes, they are. The reverse is also true. Some of the noblest minds/souls/embodiments present a shy, almost insignificant image to the world. Perhaps intrinsic humility inspires them to protect their hidden beauty.

Ruth Bader Ginsburg comes to mind.
Although President Jimmy Carter appointed her to the Court of Appeals in 1980, it took another 13 years before Justice was given justice. Seldom has so much *"sound and light"* remained hidden *"in sacred biochemical garments"* for so long. She was already 60 years old when President Clinton became aware of her talents and appointed her to the position of Associate Justice of the U.S. Supreme Court.
A most exceptional human being.
Not Clinton but Ginsburg.

As for Einstein's *bundles of frequencies*, we have to accept the fact that our brain and heart are 73% water. Our lungs are about 83%, which probably dates back to when we were still fish that emerged from primordial slime bubbling at the hydrothermal vents. For better or for worse, by now, we occupy bodies that, on average, are only 60% water.
I don't put that much even in my Scotch.
Is this what you feel you are? 60% water? Or... perhaps Einstein was right. We are just an illusion. The real "WE" are invisible and quite dry.

Nevertheless, Being & Becoming are the two faces of reality. The unchangeable, indestructible, inexhaustible Cause, and the eternally metamorphosing Result. Most people prefer to ignore the first. They don't seem aware that the moment the Energy of Consciousness leaves their bodies they 'die'. Or they think they die. Their illusory, transient, ephemeral physical hosts are no longer Becoming. The Being part of their individuality moved on to realities of higher vibrations.

Such realities most of us can only experience in our dreams. (Don't forget how many people find their inspiration in their dreams. I most certainly do.)

That's right. We cannot die.

Energy of Consciousness is indestructible. Even individualized Consciousness, such as we are, goes on. After all, it remains inseparable from Its Source. From the Energy of Omnipresent Consciousness.

Yet, having said all that, we must never forget the purpose and the importance of our Becoming. It is only by the realization of new ideas through our phenomenal awareness, or by the memories created by the actions stimulated by the artificial intelligence generated by our biological computer (brain), that we can add to the reality of the phenomenal Universe.

Why does it matter?

Because until such takes place, the Being aspect remains only a theoretical, intangible reality. Only through the evolution leading to the creation and development of a complex entity such as a human being, equipped with a brain capable of generating artificial consciousness, that the manifestation of the phenomenal Universe can be increased. While the Potential of the Energy of Omnipresent Consciousness is infinite, it does not follow that the present totality of the phenomenal Universe can absorb all the new ideas.

"We", or our "*ego consciousness*" tests new ideas through trial and error procedures. Hence, insignificant though we are in the infinity of the scheme of things, we are indispensable to the expansion of the phenomenal Universe. Evelyn Monahan thus describes our nature:

"I am a magnificent human being. I am without equal in all creation. My mind and body are so magnificently constructed that no feat of engineering could ever duplicate the uniqueness in myself. I will transcend all ordinary thinking and dwell entirely in my higher self.

In the awareness of my higher self I know no limits. My will is the strongest force in all of creation. I will now to be in ever-increasing contact with my higher self." [1]

I'll probably repeat this statement, because it needs repeating. We do not seem to be aware what incredible constructs our bodies are. Also, this, in my opinion, is as close as one can get to the *"Ye are gods"* expression. And let us never forget that this process is ongoing, and it continues to enhance the Universe on the eternal path to Infinity.

Hence, in a way, for an ephemeral fraction of time, the Consciousness of Being and Becoming are *One*.

Aren't we lucky?

Regretfully, not everyone agrees with Evelyn Monahan. Between "What we are" and "What we *really* are", there is a gap of ignorance, greed, and stupidity. Yet, to continue enhancing the Universe, we must look after our 'illusory' bodies. We can rely on cooperating with our immune system developed over millions if not billions of years, or we can fall back on our artificial intelligence which produced our 'modern' medicine, or medicine as we know it, which started to emerge in the late 18th century, after the Industrial Revolution.

Frankly, I don't like the odds.

In his book, *THE BODY* (mentioned in Chapter 3),[2]

CONCLUSIONS

Bill Bryson assures us that human stupidity can lead to our demise. Some of us recall the celebrations we (well, some of us) had when Sir Alexander Fleming was awarded the Nobel Prize for the discovery of penicillin. Since that time, instead of relying on their own healing powers, let alone on our immune system, people, at the slightest pretext, consumed, or injected themselves, with antibiotics.

And this was not only the consequence of the stupidity of parents who, at the slightest pretext, probably out of fear, insisted on antibiotic treatment for their children on every occasion. This was encouraged by the unadulterated greed of the pharmaceutical and medical professions, who fulfilled the ignorant parents' requests for the sole reason of making money. Either that, or abject ignorance, for which they still charged money.

In addition, the pharmaceutical and farming industries fed, and continue to feed, their livestock with an abundance of antibiotics, which were later consumed by carnivorous nature of the ignorant masses. This food chain led to the gradual diminution of resistance to any bacteria that may have attacked human bodies. When we, humans, obsessed with eating meat, consumed vast amounts of it, we also swallowed bacteria which, over time, had already become quite immune to the penicillin and other antibiotics.

Unfortunately, there are no antibiotics or any other medications that might protect us from the pandemic diseases of greed and stupidity.

> *"In 1945 when Alexander Fleming won the Nobel Prize, a typical case of pneumococcal pneumonia could be knocked out with 40 thousand units of penicillin. Today, because of increased resistance, it can take more than twenty million units per day, for many days, to achieve the same results."*[2]

I find it quite amazing what a combination of stupidity

and greed can achieve in such a short time. Let us hope that the Age of Aquarius will bring about a little enlightenment.

Yet what remains, is a more fundamental problem. Animals left to themselves, without negative influences of us, humans, tend to live lives assigned to them by nature. Their immune system takes care of external influences, but most of all, protects the whole species, more so than its individual members.

Not so with humans.

We tend to abuse the natural laws. We overeat, are often too sedentary, and generally ignore the common sense that nature assigned to us. Instead, we spend millions of dollars on trying to produce chemicals to repair the damage we have done by disobeying what our nature dictates. We often spend millions of dollars on unsuccessful attempts to cure people, who should never have succumbed to any diseases.

Instead of learning the laws that control and or protect our lives, we learn how to repair the damage we inflict on our bodies through dire ignorance or just weakness of character.

Shouldn't that change?

We seem to forget that we are not our bodies. That our bodies are wonderful gifts given to us out of the generosity of the Universe, to enjoy, and to enhance the Universe with diversity and gratitude. Once we accept this premise, our diseases will gradually diminish to the frequencies we observe in other species.

So... WHAT ARE WE?

Well, some of us are just beginning to perceive that we are more than flesh and bones. Others, the vast majority, rely on their bodies to create a reality in which they want to live. A fairly abortive endeavour. Hence, it is their bodies they are trying to enhance.

Superficially.

Many women spend small fortunes on painting their faces all sorts of unnatural colours. Not just their lips but eyes, cheeks, overall epidermis, in addition to changing the colour of their hair, nails, and whatever else they can think of. Obviously, they do not believe that nature's evolutionary process has done them justice.

In addition to all of the above, they treat themselves as out-of-season Xmas-trees, by hanging a variety of colorful, preferably shiny objects on their necks, ears, often eyebrows, noses, and wherever else they imagine the opposite sex would find them attractive. And all this in addition to whatever plastic surgery has to offer.

Men go beyond the epidermis.

Nature laboured for a few million years to provide us with a smooth, abrasion-resistant skin that can repair itself in a relatively short time. Ultimately, nature succeeded so well, that a thick coating of protective fur was no longer required. The ladies of our species seemed to appreciate nature's efforts. They, more so than men, appear to admire the smoothness of their silky skin.

Men, on the other hand, seemed dissatisfied with nature's efforts.

They may have given up most of the skin painting jobs which their predecessors did until recently, and instead, proceeded to cover their often obese bodies with a multitude of tattoos. They apply this dubious art form not just to their faces, but disfigure most parts of their bodies in a profoundly elaborate fashion. I have no idea if they do it to attract the opposite sex, or repel it, or merely to cover the perceived inadequacies of appearance and thus boost their fragile egos.

However, *de gustibus non disputandum est*.

This applies to both sexes of the species.

In addition, men do all this pseudo-artistic rigmarole while flexing their muscles in, presumably, a provocative manner. Obviously they think that women prefer muscle to brain. Perhaps they are right. After all, to each his and her own?

Evidently, the female of the species must find such appearance and behaviour attractive, or the population of *homo no-longer-sapiens* would not grow at such an alarming rate.

Yet, lately, the devolution took another step downward, and the most incredible thing happened. Women, the silky-skinned beautiful women, began to copy men in their skin-destroying maneuvers. They, too, began to destroy their beauty with tattoos.

Please, don't get me wrong. I am not against makeup. I like makeup to enhance the Universe I live in. And if a woman enhances her features to make herself more beautiful, I'm all for it. What I am against is when she denies millions of years of evolution and changes her appearance beyond recognition hiding her face behind a mask of a clown. All right... Not all women. But even one would be too many.

After all, I also shave and have an occasional haircut. There are two reasons for it. The first is that my wife insists that I do so. And the second, a close call behind, is that I have no desire to look like a poor imitation of an insipid gorilla. I enjoy being human. I might as well try to look like one.

Only please, *no* tattoos. After all, gorillas don't have them, either.

Of one thing we can be sure. Even if quite a few of us may have risen above the *'Third Party"*, and have already joined the membership of the "*Many that are called*", this group, now, seems to be regressing. To date, they have perfunctorily dismissed the idea that they might be hosts to an immortal 'being' (an immortal state of Consciousness), who or which is desperately trying to be heard from within their hearts.

Yes, not brains, not even minds, but hearts.

It is the feeling they are missing, not a prescient mental calculation of what they might or might not be. Women have less of such problems. They have greater capacity and ability to listen to their emotions. To their hearts. They need them to be mothers.

A motherly love is an incredibly powerful energy.

As for men, the sad part is that the glorious guests they are harboring within can do nothing until the hosts are willing to acknowledge their presence. The 'guests' who happen to be their creators. Yet, the guests cannot leave... (though they are probably desperately trying to get out). It seems that the vast majority of us are still in the reactive mode.

After all, we are all still in the kindergarten!

So much for our appearance; for our physical attributes; for our bodies. Please note that there are always the Few who refuse to regress to the primitive mode of behaviour of the majority. I'm sure you're one of the Few or you would have stopped reading my elegy by now.

Or... am I completely wrong on all counts?

Perhaps a completely new species is evolving beyond my ability to recognize it?

A biological robot in the image and likeness of something else altogether? An admix of biological and technological cyborgs?

You decide.

One may have thought that beauty, by whatever name, could only be within or without, but not both. On the other hand, this would preclude all nature from having an inner beauty, which concept I refuse to accept. The only solution is for the two to become One. Haven't we heard this before?

"*I and my father are One*"...

And now, a word about the character we reached after seven million years of evolution. Recently, I watched David Attenborough's film about the jungle. Essentially, it confirmed my suspicions that, in the jungle, everybody eats everybody. They used to call it the food-chain. Supposedly, we are at the very top of it, although our medical profession assures us that we continue to be gustatory delight of trillions of microorganisms—not only the epidermal dust we leave behind whenever we walk, but the millions of tidbits we offer them in our digestive system.

Bon apétitte!
Some things never change?

Apparently, this jungle culinary *mélange* applies to all of the animal kingdom with which David acquaintained us.

But then came a chocking surprise.

Climbing the evolutionary ladder, Sir David Frederick Attenborough moved on to monkeys. I stress his title and full name to differentiate him from the object of his exposition. Why? Because they, the nearest and dearest of our predecessors, the hominids, fought and killed their own kind to expand their territory.

Reminds you of anyone? Are we so far apart?

Ken Follett, the author of *The Fall of Giants*, puts another slant on this mode of behaviour:

> "*Men were the only animals that slaughtered their own kind by the million, and turned the landscape into a waste of shell craters and barbed wire. Perhaps the human race would wipe itself out*

completely, and leave the world to the birds and trees... Perhaps that would be for the best."

Were...? Or are we still? Today?

As for monkeys, to maintain their superiority over other great apes, or where they monkeys (?), they not only murdered but ate the children of their competing tribe.

Is this our immediate past?

Or, as Ken Follett observes, considering the devolutionary trend in our behaviour pattern, our foreseeable future? It might be, if our illustrious leaders argued that such menu would reduce hunger in the world. And, observing the human jungle, our benevolent leaders will argue anything to get reelected.

And why do I raise this subject? Because it brings me to another dilemma. Why wasn't Jesus a vegan, or at least a vegetarian? Surely, he was the most compassionate man on Earth. We know that he surrounded himself with fishermen, but, we are told, he also ate meat. We know that he favoured fish meals, but, surely, at Passover a lamb had to be slaughtered ceremoniously.

I draw two possible conclusions.

One, that he didn't want to upset the customs of the day more than necessary, or two, that he favoured the Buddhist approach.

> *"According to Theravada, the **Buddha** allowed his monks to **eat pork, chicken** and **fish** if the monk was aware that the animal was not killed on their behalf."*
>
> Buddhist vegetarianism
(Wikipedia)

A logical sentiment of *"waste not, want not."*

In order to finish with the subject, I revert, once more, to Albert Einstein. He seems to argue that only the creative act is real. *All else is an illusion.* Even the fish are not real. On the other hand, if the Jains[(3)] are right, and the evolutions works in cycles, then soon we might all revert to being monkeys, and eat our neighbours' children.

I am reminded of the American comedian, actor, juggler, and writer, W.C. Fields, who once stated: *"I like children. If they're properly cooked."* We can only hope that the misanthropic egoist wasn't prophetic in his contemptuous observation!

Although, would it be so much worse than murdering millions of people, members of the same species, by dropping bombs on them from thirty thousand feet?

After all, in a way, we already, or still, are cannibals. We may not eat our own species any more, but we most certainly eat the species we were a little while ago.

And yet, after all, we too, started in Paradise, in the Garden of Eden. At least Adam did. And, reputedly, we all have divine potential within us. And... look at us now.

You decide.

~~~

(1) Evelyn M. Monahan, *The Miracle of Metaphysical Healing.*
(2) Bill Bryson, *The Body.*
(3) Jainism is a non-theistic religion founded in India in the 6th century BC.

Chapter 11
ALL IS ENERGY
(The God Diffusion)

> *"It is important to realize that in physics today, we have no knowledge of what energy is."*
> **Richard P. Feynman (1918 - 1988)**
> Nobel Prize in Physics (1965)

> *"There is enough energy in a single cubic meter of space to boil all the oceans in the world."*
> **Richard P. Feynman (1918 - 1988)**

> *"All gods are homemade, and it is we who pull their strings, and so, give them the power to pull ours."*
> **Aldous Leonard Huxley, (1894 - 1963)**
> British Author

The sentiment expressed in this Chapter has already been offered on a number of occasions. I continue repeating it as, for countless generations, we, the human species, have been conditioned to think of things, of objects, of matter... as real. And indeed, for as long as we regard them as such, such objects remain real. Our primitive senses define our reality.

Sorry, Albert, be it energy or matter, my friends still refuse to accept it as illusion.

Yet, when we encounter those very same objects in our dreams, they assume quite different qualities. There, in that "other" reality, we can walk through walls, levitate, swim at length under the water, and even fly. I'm sure we've all experienced at least one or two of such feats.

If you do not recall your dreams, I suggest that you keep a notebook on your bedside table, and the moment you wake up, jot down whatever you *can* recall. It may be just a word or two, but in time you'll train your mind to improve mental access to your subconscious, where all your memories are stored.

Your own dreams will surprise you.

For at least the last few millennia, and for most of us until fairly recently, God was responsible for our lives, our things, our actions. If we were good and obeyed His Commandments, we were rewarded. If we were not 'good', we were punished, and not just here and now but, believe it or not, for ever and ever. God was obviously a most incredibly unforgiving sadist.

Or...

Or the religious preachers were, and are, abysmally wrong. The mystics of the past tried to set them right, but all of them were studiously ignored.

On the other hand, regardless of divine humour, there are consequences to all our actions. And even our thoughts. Be they 'good' or 'bad'. Not good or bad for you or your friends, but for the Universe. They expanded and enhanced our reality—or they didn't.

At any rate, they are just consequences. Surely, that's fair enough, isn't it?

It is called *karma*.

And then we were saved. Not by a flabbergasting miracle, nor any divine revelation, but by Albert Einstein. He, as already mentioned, declared that *all is energy*, and even worse, *all is illusion*. It didn't help that Richard Feynman insisted that we have no idea what energy is. It may be Consciousness or what our parents called Spirit. What's in a name, as Shakespeare would say; what does it matter what we call It?

But surely, not God!

Well, even that depends on what we mean by God. After all, Einstein wanted to know His thoughts. Was that an illusion, too? Actually, it would have been if we thought of God as a very, very, very powerful man.

Luckily He, She, or It isn't. Isn't human, I mean. On the other hand, aren't we all gods?

Note... the small 'g'.

The word simply refers to the Creative Power.

Also, luckily, according to some great prophets, mystics, and even the Messiah, God is in Heaven, and Heaven is within us. Yes, within you and me. And everyone. In fact, the Creative Energy of Consciousness, which we regard as God, is omnipresent. Hence, there is no such place where It isn't.

Omnipresence is an absolute.

And then, there is another paradox. It seems that It (*i.e.*, God) is neither good nor bad. At least, not by human standards. After all, aren't human standards quite flexible? Ask any politician. Or the religious fraternity. Have you heard about Holy Wars? We just killed our friends; killing enemies had been forbidden.

There appear to be only two prerequisites that define the Universal concept of "good", and we seem to be responsible for both of them.

The first is *Expansion*, and the second is *Singularity*.

The expansion happens when we contribute something new to the phenomenal Universe. The Singularity, however, assures that the Universe remains One.

A continuous expansion of the Single Universe. Of the Single, Omnipresent Consciousness.

There are two collateral aspects to this definition. Expansion is the primary cause of centrifugal forces, whereas the prerequisite of Singularity produces its centripetal equivalent. Hence: the two qualities that define what is good. All other attributes of the reality of the phenomenal Universe are a direct collateral of these primary two.

The way Richard Feynman talks of energy, it seems that it has much greater potential, or power, than we previously suspected. In fact, only the religious concept of spirit, of spiritual energy, might be comparable to the efficacy he assigns to energy, although, also according to him, we have no knowledge of what energy is.

After all, it seems to emerge from Black Holes, and nobody, neither priest nor scientist, has the slightest idea what's inside of these... whatever they are.
And yet Einstein, his fellow Nobel Prize recipient in Physics, defines all reality as energy. Is this where science and religions meet? Is energy—the energy of Spirit, the omnipresent energy of Consciousness—all there is?
You decide.
I know that, like Socrates, I know nothing.

CONCLUSIONS   115

Chapter 12
KNOWLEDGE WITHIN
(The End of the Beginning)

> *"Diplomacy is the art of telling people to go to hell in such a way that they ask for directions."*
> **Winston Churchill (1874 - 1965)**
> British Wartime Prime Minister

> *"Politics is not the art of the possible. It consists in choosing between the disastrous and the unpalatable."*
> **John Kenneth Galbraith, (1908 - 2006)**
> Canadian-American economist and author

> *"See that the imagination of nature is far, far greater than the imagination of man."*
> **Richard P. Feynman (1918 - 1988)**
> American physicist,
> recipient of joint Nobel Prize in Physics in 1965.

There are many ways in which we can share, in fact spread, or disseminate, knowledge that, according to Winston Churchill, might well lead us to Hell. There is, however, a wonderful consolation to this premise. The only knowledge the diplomats, politicians, and even the scientists can spread, no matter how politely, how surreptitiously, is knowledge dealing with the phenomenal reality, which we already know is *not* real.

Yet politicians and diplomats have found a way to convey their views to both, their friends and enemies. Such knowledge may be destructive to the listener, no matter how amicable it sounds. Let us never forget that Hell, just like Heaven, is a state of Consciousness.

On the other hand, every single piece of knowledge we obtain from within, from our unconscious, is *always*, without a single exception, for our good!

Amazing?

As mentioned, every one of us was created for the sole purpose of enhancing and adding to the diversity of the phenomenal Universe. The ancients described our phenomenal reality as Paradise. As the Garden of Eden. We could have stayed there if our Egos hadn't aspired to knowledge which, we thought, would translate into power.

Some of us didn't think so. Some of us preferred to forsake power and other exigencies of Ego and channel our abilities to the original purpose.

They, and they alone, count among the *Few*.

For those Few, the creative process is everything. Please note: the *process*, not the result. After all, it's the whole world, the whole Cosmos, that they have to enhance. For the Greeks, the Universe already was a thing of beauty. *Cosmos,*[1] in Greek, means not only 'order' or "arrangement", but "adornment". We might well ask, "adornment" of what? And the only answer that comes to mind is the manifestation of our 'Consciousness'. Our awareness. In a way, if we had been created to abide in the Garden of Eden, then that would have been our *"raison d'être"*. The reason why we are alive. The preoccupation with surrounding our phenomenal life with beauty.

Like Paradise?

It is still there. And here. Within our state of Consciousness, waiting to be discovered. For those who sit back, or go once a week to their place of worship to ask their God to do things for them, the Bible will be a terrible disappointment.

All knowledge we gain from others, while it may improve our own lives, does not contribute to additional diversity. It can still be positive, a means to an end; but, regrettably, the end would be transient and illusory. Only the enchantment of Consciousness has lasting power. It becomes immortal.

And yet we have been given precise instructions regarding both, method and consequences:

> *"Whatsoever a man soweth, that shall he also reap."*
>
> Galatians (6:7)

> *"For verily I say unto you, till heaven and earth pass, one jot or one tittle shall in no wise pass from the law, till all be fulfilled."*
>
> Matthew (5:18)

> *"And it is easier for heaven and earth to pass, than one tittle of the law to fail."*
>
> Luke (16:17)

The Bible is replete with information telling how we can recreate the Garden of Eden, a veritable Paradise on Earth. Only we have to do it ourselves. We cannot wait for some imaginary deity to do it for us. This is not a valley of tears.

This is a reality of joy.

Of joy abounding within us, waiting to be released and manifested in the phenomenal reality. It doesn't even have to be real. We just must perceive it as real. After all, it already exists within us.

~~~

(1) The Greek word *Cosmos* means "order" or "arrangement"; it may also mean "adornment". It refers to the Universe, *i.e.*: the whole of creation.

Chapter 13
TIME
(Why We Are: Phase Two)
[This question is an on-going discussion)

> *"It has been said that we have not had the three R's in America, we had the six R's: remedial readin', remedial 'ritin' and remedial 'rithmetic."*
> **Robert Maynard Hutchins, (1899–1977)**
> Educational philosopher,

> *"In nature there are neither rewards nor punishments; there are consequences."*
> **Robert Green Ingersoll (1833-1899)**
> American social activist, orator and agnostic

> *"There is nothing permanent except change."*
> **Heraclitus (....... - 475 BC)**
> Pre-Socratic Ionian Greek philosopher

We neither were, nor will be. WE ARE. Or at least we are as individuals from the moment we have been 'individualized', although our essential nature hasn't changed. We have not changed our nature, our basic character, since the moment we became embodiments of the Omnipresent Consciousness. Like points in physics, discussed in the Introduction and in Chapter 20.

Nevertheless, let us get back to the phenomenal dimension of time. Yes, phenomenal dimension, hence it is not real. It is an illusion. Albeit, as Einstein would say, a *"very persistent one"*.

The problem of time is gravely misunderstood. In the true reality, there is only the eternal present. One might call

it Omnipresent. God, whatever this word symbolizes to you, neither was, nor will be, but IS. Neither here nor there but everywhere.
An eternal stasis.
Hence the need for the phenomenal reality. It introduces the concept of eternal life, or the State of Consciousness in the eternal state of amorphosis.

There is only one purpose for our lives. We are intended to diversify and enhance the Universe. Not our own wellbeing, nor even our neighbours', but the Universe's. Of course, the two may be complementary. After all, each one of us is inseparable from the totality of the Universe.

Unfortunately this commission did not come with a set of implicit instructions. In fact, (as already mentioned) to assure that diversification will bring new qualities into the phenomenal Universe, the Energy of Creative Consciousness brought the concept of evolution into the phenomenal reality. This, in fact, eventually led to the magnificent biological construct we call men.

Who knows how many equal, or greatly more advanced amorphous instruments capable of converting the potential into a phenomenal expression populate the vastness of the continuously expanding phenomenal Universe. The Energy of Consciousness is Infinite, hence must be Its expression.

World without end!

THE SCHOOL

[As I did with KINDERGARTEN, I include these excerpts adapted from Beyond Religion 1, Essay #52. As THE SCHOOL provides answers rather than raising questions, I include it for people who may not have had a chance to read DELUSIONS—

Pragmatic Realism. If you are already familiar with it, please move onto the next chapter.]

During this phase of evolution, the human entity develops advanced communication skills and becomes susceptible to the influences of theoretical knowledge. It learns to be selective in its relationship to the Universal Laws governing its environment.

In the 'School', the teachers are responsible for the efficacy of imparting knowledge to their pupils. During this evolutionary phase, the units of Consciousness are organized within a variety of classrooms. The purpose of this tendency towards aggregations is to extend the awareness of the Self beyond its space/time confines, *i.e.:* beyond its internal and the adjacent external environment. The classrooms consist of groups within which the Self reaches out to include the allegiances to families, clans, villages, towns, religious congregations and national formations—with which the Self can identify.

This is not limited to the human species.

In order to facilitate control over the nascent units of Consciousness, the 'teachers' (those who usurped authority) endeavour to maintain their subjects in abject ignorance. We are taught that obedience—to those in power—is a virtue. Regrettably, with few exceptions, the teachers are also ignorant of the true reality. The rare Avatars (invariably non-conformists and in direct opposition to the prevailing *status quo*) cast seeds of wisdom on the developing states of individualized Consciousness. The seeds seldom strike fertile soil. More often than not, they meet an inflexible mindset bent on protecting rather than improving acquired knowledge. Other seeds reach receptive minds, but are stifled by the orthodox establishment in control. The few who break with traditions are ridiculed, often persecuted, sometimes killed. Those wielding power strongly discourage free thought and individuality.

The last segment of this phase is characterized by rebellion (The Age of Aquarius). We gradually lose faith in our 'teachers'. We observe countless contradictions between their teaching and their behaviour pattern. This dichotomy is particularly in evidence within the sacerdotal and political ranks. We still obey, mostly due to inbred fear, but simultaneously begin to strike out on our own.

This invariably leads to a period of apostasy that results in achieving a degree of freedom from previous conditioning. When we feel secure, we begin to compare the various teachings, each claiming absolute exclusivity over truth. This is factual of all religions, all branches of science, and all other sources of authority. The religious tithing may bleed us just as easily, as leeches applied to our skin by scientists, as by governments which send us to fight their battles.

Please note, it is always *their* battles.

At this stage of our development, my (previous, and still illustrious) hero, the distinguished expert on biological evolution, proposes an interesting supposition. He suggests that religion may fit into the same branch of learning as conditioning of young children, in order to procure from them absolute obedience, and thus, in time of need, save their lives. For evolutionary biologists, physical survival is a *sine qua non* condition of evolution. This is not the case with regard to the evolution of Consciousness, which essentially is indestructible.

Perhaps I should mention, once more, Richard Dawkins. While his expertise in evolutionary biology is undeniable, his attack on the Bible is closely reminiscent of Don Quixote de la Mancha's irrepressible battles with the windmills. Both have no idea what, or even why, they are fighting shadows of their ignorance.

Even so, while Dawkins's proposal may indeed save one or two retarded youngsters, I have personal experience of parents *teaching*—not *training*—their children, to get the same effect. While soldiers are trained to obey orders unquestioningly, children should question theirs, very early, and have them explained. This is strictly against religious teaching, which relies on faith rather than knowledge, in the old days referred to as *gnosis*. Although *gnosis* is defined in the dictionary as "knowledge of spiritual mysteries", I'd prefer to place the accent on the word *knowledge*, and substitute Pragmatic Realism for "spiritual mysteries".

After all, this is what all the ancient mystics were attempting to fathom.

By this method (teaching rather than training), the children mature much faster, "and can cross the road without an old man/woman holding up the traffic". The children, not having been taught to look both ways before crossing, rely exclusively on the commands of the supervisor. A lot like soldiers. It makes the young-ones mentally retarded at a very early age. By the same token should soldiers refuse to act without thinking, I dare suggests their action would cut our wars in half, or at least the collateral damage would be virtually eliminated. Not the order to 'duck' only to 'fire'.

This, surely, must be the fundamental difference between reactive Darwinism and a proactive educational approach. What may work for bugs, does not necessarily work for primates, and possibly for other mammals.

If Pragmatic Realism is taken into consideration, then we must ask ourselves if what worked for primitive life-forms could possibly work for (hopefully) thinking creatures. Recently, I often had more intelligent responses from cats and dogs, than from members of our government who relied on outdated traditions. This is most probably due to the unquestionable fact that early conditioning is very hard to get rid of. In my own case, it took me almost twenty years of concentrated, very conscious effort, to free myself from my early religious upbringing.

We are also at present witnessing the near-permanent mental and emotional damage inflicted by the imposed obedience on thousands of veterans of the Iraq war. The same is true of most "armed conflicts". The moment man stops thinking, ultimately he pays for it. We can no longer continue to blame Darwin's theories of natural selection. None of us have been selected to be obedient and stupid. We acquired these traits solely by ourselves.

As for those at the other end of the equation, those whose job is to lead, who may have been attracted like moths to the deadly flame of power, we can say NO. Let them lead by example, by reason, not by imposing unquestioning obedience.

The weak use the carrot and the stick.
The strong always lead by example.

In School we take our first tentative steps on our own, outside our comfort zone. In time we discover that if we eliminate ninety-nine percent of the miasma that our teachers (leaders, politicians, preachers, priests, parents, elders) have imposed on the *original* teachings of a variety of Great Masters of the past, the residual essence is virtually the same from all sources of wisdom. We begin to suspect that if all the great Avatars taught the same *a priori* knowledge, then there must be an original source from which they, the Avatars, drew their wisdom.

We begin searching for the source.

In time, we discover that our physical bodies are what

we use, *inter alia*, to exercise our ability to move from place to place in pursuit of satisfying our needs. We discover that it is not the body that propels us, as in kindergarten, but it is our will that propels our body. Our attention shifts from being motivated by the material, internal and external environment, to that of mental and emotional attributes.

We develop conscious awareness of our Self. The most efficient way of achieving this aim is to change our attitude from reactive to proactive. This, of course, entails responsibility.

But there are problems.

Lack of responsibility manifested by most people in charge is the main problem associated with this phase. I shall limit myself to the subject of education, though similar shortcomings can be found of all other aspects of our society. The juvenile behaviour of senators and representatives in Washington is an ample example of that. Members of various parliaments are not far behind.

In addition to my notes above about the teachers, there is also a small number of them who try to meet their obligations. Nevertheless, the education system has changed even the language we use to accommodate our shortcomings. We began calling pupils 'students', and teachers 'professors'. This change in nomenclature may be flattering to both parties, but also leads to distortion of the function which both of them are intended to perform.

A student studies, a pupil is being taught.

A student decides what he or she wishes to study—a pupil must conform to a curriculum. A professor delivers a discourse, a teacher conducts a lesson, deciding what the pupils are to learn and when.

We seldom find teachers who assume full responsibility for their pupils' level of advancement. It is true that parents

CONCLUSIONS

of limited intelligence tend to impose restrictions on the means teachers can employ in their teaching, but the consequences are a general malaise in the educational system.

Furthermore, the teachers are deprived of being able to impose any form of discipline on the children (the pupils), and thus can hardly be held responsible for lack of results. Under the circumstances, in order to protect their jobs, teachers are, more or less, forced to lower the 'pass' standards of their classes. The consequence of this 'educational' system results in hordes of 'graduates' unable to read or write.

Those juvenile delinquents are then picked up by colleges of "higher learning" on the so-called sports scholarships, and eventually they enter the adult world with virtually no general knowledge, often with inordinate amounts of money, and their bodies full of steroids.

Parenthetically, in the first decade of this millennium, in the USA, rookies in professional basketball were paid between $800,000 and $2 million a year. Their average income would rise to $10 million a year, while the 'stars' would exceed $25 million. With endorsements, this figure can surpass $35 million annual income. Michael Jordan is said to have earned that much in 2004. Ability to read or write is not a requirement. In baseball, their poor cousins make, on average, only $3 million per year. The premier league professional soccer players in the UK are not far behind.

Just to sate your interest, an average annual income of a neurosurgeon for an average of 40 hours a week (2080-hour year), as calculated by the US Government Bureau of Labor Statistics, comes to $219,770, with the upper 10% reaching or even exceeding $300,000. Jackson & Coker's (the physician recruitment firm) survey of a median neurosurgeon salary in the Northeast of the US places it at around

$500,000. Almost one-twentieth of an average baseball player salary, or one-fortieth of the better ones. Next time you have a brain tumor I suggest you use a baseball bat.

Notwithstanding any of the above, to be fair, I must mention that there are the "FEW" (from the *"Many that were called"*) who donate large sums of money to charitable causes. While this is fairly common among sportsmen at the top of their professions, and some actors, I'm at a loss to find equal generosity among the multimillion-dollar politicians, although even among them philanthropy is not unheard of.

By the way, elementary school instructors average $50,500; about one/two-hundredth of an average baseball player. Good luck with your children.

This absurd disparity between the compensations awarded in professional sports and other non-producing industries is a powerful stimulus for the young to give up education in the pursuit of easier *modi vivendi*.

Third-rate acting on TV is another option, although they are usually expected to know how to read.

Until this matter is regulated and teachers (and not administrators or even parents) become, once again, in full charge of education, the level of pupils' acumen will continue to cascade downwards. Regardless of the teachers' income.

At present, the schooling system (barring some exceptions) is suggestive of devolution. One must also remember what I mentioned in Chapter 6—Phase Two. It is imperative that we, humans, harmonize the process of natural selection, with the evolutionary process. Regrettably, to date, our efforts tend to weaken even our responses to diseases; we rely more and more on chemicals to supplement our immune system developed over millions of years. One could blame the biochemical conglomerates for their inordinate greed; but they, too, consist of individual people who appear to practice the Darwinian creed (actually coined by the British philosopher Herbert Spencer) of the "survival of the fittest," or, at the very least, the richest.

Or greediest?

Recently I heard on the News, that more people die prematurely as the consequence of excessive use of *prescription* drugs than die of cocaine and heroin combined. If true, it doesn't say much for the evolutionary development of our medical profession.

Still, in SCHOOL we are supposed to learn, no matter what the cost. Regrettably, few of us do. Hence, devolution.

Finally, I am often surprised that biologists limit their religious proclivities, or more often lack of them, to Darwinian precepts. Noble and pragmatic though they may be, they (I assume rightly) exclude divine intervention from dipping its fingers into the evolutionary stew—I mean process. The word 'divine' can be interpreted in any number of non-religious ways. I've met women who were simply divine.

Some desserts I've had…

Basically, anyone acting proactively, as against reactively, can be considered to act in a divine manner. It is the non-Darwinian, or proactive, ethic that stops us from imposing our natural sexual instincts on the opposite sex.

In the Darwinian sense, this is wasteful and non-productive. In this context, the statement by George Bernard Shaw, *"The fact that a believer is happier than a skeptic is no more to the point than the fact that a drunken man is happier than a sober one,"* is particularly erroneous. There is a very fundamental difference (I hate that word…). The believer may be happier than a skeptic by having examined both sides of the equation and having chosen the one which pleased him/her more. The same is true of the opposite conclusion, of course. He/she had made a *conscious* decision. A drunken man is in no position to make conscious decisions of any nature. He, or his biological makeup, reacts to the stimulus of alcohol. He is a slave to his urges, unable to make a balanced decision—no more so than any animal responding to its conditioning. Thus, he has no idea if he's happy or not.

He is held in a reactive, not a proactive, behaviour.

I have been told that a pair of cats can produce 500 kittens within a period of two years. The question is, should they? Can the environment in which they do so support their progeny? Like a drunken man, they no more than react to their conditioning.

They don't care.

Nor does a drunken man. But what of his happiness when he sobers up?

I am yet to discover what universal forces, or laws, the evolutionary biologists hold responsible for lack of evolution (not life, only evolution), on the Moon, Mars, Venus, Saturn, and other places of interplanetary interest. Does natural selection begin only when there is something to select? If not, what was non-evolving before the evolution began? Or, simply, what does one select? Was it all a lucky accident? Or is there an inherent energy, a property, in the matrix of the Universe that precipitates the onset of the evolutionary process—like a number of other universal laws espoused by physicists. It seems to me that theoretical physicists are much more creative in inventing laws that suit their purposes—whatever those might be.

There is another aspect of our psyche that undergoes evolution during this stage. For the first time, we, the nascent individuals, consider the question of dualism of our reality. I do not just mean up-and-down, black-and-white, hot-and-cold. What I am referring to is the dualism which we detect in our own nature. This manifests in the recognition of both the physical and non-physical aspects of our being. I suspect that evolutionary biologists would tend to assign all non-physical aspects of our makeup to be strictly reactive. Our non-physical makeup is variously defined as our emotions, psyche, mind, spirit, soul, id, atma, and possibly a number of other, more esoteric terms.

Biologists refer to those who recognize both aspects of their nature as dualists. The scientists define them as people who separate their mind from their body. The other group are referred to as monists. Usually, the scientists regard themselves as monists, as, indeed, I consider myself. From the pragmatic point of view, I have no choice but to consider myself a monist.

There is a problem, though.

Most monistic scientists regard matter as the only reality. They believe, and it is definitely an act of faith, that mind is the product of the brain, which has developed, over millions, perhaps billions of years, from an amoeba. I could go further back, but there is no need to confuse the issue. As for this group of monists, in a way, you might say that they regard themselves as very advanced amoebae.

Well, to each his own. Her own?

I repeat I, too, am a monist. But I have never been an amoeba. I have, some time ago, used the rudimentary biological structure of an amoeba to find my expression in the dualistic reality; but my reality, my real awareness, has always resided in the freedom of monistic reality. I have always been, and continue to be, an indivisible part of a ubiquitous mind: intangible, non-judgmental, timeless, ubiquitous mind.

I prefer to define it as a Consciousness. Mind, usually, performs a function. Consciousness just is, though it seems to contain infinite attributes waiting to be discovered.

The French philosopher, René Descartes, once defined his being by the fact that he 'thought' himself capable of thought. Of thinking. We all know the phrases:
"Je pense donc je suis." "Cogito ergo sum." "I think, therefore I am."

This admonition is known in every language under the sun. What is not known is that not many people show evidence that they think. Judging by their behaviour, no more so than an amoeba. No more than is required of them to stay "alive". Well, an advanced amoeba. But, surely, those people still *are*, aren't they?

And here we enter the pragmatic essence of the illusion of dualism. Monists, my type of monists, are people who do not differentiate between the reality of being and becoming. The *being* aspect is static, undifferentiated from the omnipresent Consciousness. The *becoming* part is the individualization of that state. Let us never forget that, in Latin, *individual* means *indivisible*.

After millennia of scientific evolution, the scientists are beginning to reach the conclusion which the great mystics of the past tried, unsuccessfully, to share with us—the advanced amoeba?

Maya, they said. It is all an illusion...

The world, the material reality, is the product of our minds. Essentially, it is empty space. Yes, to repeat, it is 99.9999999999999% empty space. So are our brains. Even the monist scientists agree, though they are not yet ready to interpret this fact and draw pragmatic conclusions. And yet, we, the individualized states of the Omnipresent Consciousness, can use them, those highly evolved empty brains of ours, to do justice to René Descartes. Well, some of us at least try.

Chapter 14
MISUNDERSTOOD DELUSION?
(Atheist's Delusion)

"The most remarkable discovery in all of astronomy is that the stars are made of atoms of the same kind as those on the earth."
Richard P. Feynman (1918 - 1988)
American physicist,
recipient of joint Nobel Prize in Physics in 1965

"Let us have but one end in view, the welfare of humanity; and let us put aside all selfishness in consideration of language, nationality, or religion."
John Amos Comenius (1592 - 1670)
Moravian bishop, educator

All stars may be of the same atoms that we experience on Earth, only... it seems, that atoms are "all energy". As is everything. Or, we might just call it Omnipresent Energy. Of Consciousness? Or, as some have suggested in the past, just call it Spirit. Or just do your job and forget about it. Let the theoreticians theorize?

"What's in a name? That which we call a rose by any other name would smell as sweet."[1]

It really does not matter what we call it. Atheists simply do *not* believe that they are anything other than flesh and bones, or a bunch of chemicals which, by sheer accident, drew themselves together, or collapsed, to produce the (miracle of) the human body.
...which is made up of atoms... which are points in empty space.
Are atheists really empty space?

You decide.

Or do they believe that they are no more than a feeding ground for a 100 trillion microorganisms gorging themselves on their innards. Who knows what precipitates their ignorance?

Who knows? Perhaps they are. And they'll remain so until they take the next step on the evolutionary scale. Until they discover that they are more than that. How? Perhaps by looking at the seemingly gratuitous beauty of nature. Perhaps by looking at the grandeur of the night sky. Or by listening to a Beethoven's symphony or Mendelssohn's violin concerto.

Or, one day, they might just awaken.

I wish them well...

Yet the funny thing is that if you question their postulates, no matter how absurd, they raise protests, like a child whose toy is taken from them. They grasp frantically for the support of their fragile Egos, which never created anything, but merely metamorphosed the findings or observations of others, more advanced holders of Consciousnesses than their own.

Perhaps, they're simply like children?

Let us give them time...

After all, it seems that, at our present stage of our evolution, the reality we experience is, for the most part, a delusion.

What isn't? What is real?

All forms of energy.

Mostly energies that our illustrious atheists, I mean scientists, do not recognize as such. Energies generated by sources at yet beyond their reach. Like love, appreciation of beauty, humility... and many others. Energies that cannot be measured by their electronic instrumentation, yet energies that have profound effects on our reality.

Have you noticed how much longer is the shelf-life of some energies than others? We love things, let alone people, long after their physical presence is gone. As for loving ideas, concepts — such last even longer. I know people who love ideas propagated by Buddha, or Jesus, or even Moses, of thousands of years ago.

Surely such energies carry enormous power.

A man once said that no war was ever started by the perambulations of the mind, by a process of thinking. The instigating stimulus of all of them was invariably emotional. As if greed, megalomania, or just dire stupidity played on their emotions, which drove them to Ego-driven actions. Yes, all these have profound effects on our reality, no matter how transient, how illusory.

And please, make no mistake. Stupidity is a powerful energy. It makes the realities of many people go round. And round... In vicious circles.

We tend to judge others by our own standards. The Atheists' Delusions spring from their utter inability of recognizing that nothing can happen out of nothing. And if it already is something, then that something must have a beginning and an end.

Why?

Because they observe the Universe with their human senses, which are limited to seeing only that which is transient, elusive and, according to Einstein, an illusion.

And here we come to the crux of the matter. It has been written, long ago, that *"Many are called, but Few are chosen."* There is a grave omission in this premise. While the statement above is "gospel truth", it has been recorded by human, *ergo* limited knowledge. What has been omitted is the fact that the overwhelming majority of people have not, as yet, even been called. In my writing (see Chapter 2), I call them *"The Third Party"*. Even as no man, woman, or child can expect the "Second Coming" if they have not experienced the "First", neither can they can opt to join the Few if they haven't heard the "call".

The 'calling', of course, is the evolution of the awareness of the Truth. Of the true reality. The awareness must be accepted by the Artificial Intelligence generated by our brains, which is responsible for the creation of our Ego.

To admit that our Egos have limitations takes humility, and that was never an atheist's *forte*. While they deny the existence of God, they do not accept that there is a higher entity in the Universe than their own mind of which they are the proud possessors.

Yet the mind is no more than a magnificent energy capable of converting ideas generated by Self, by the individualization of the omnipresent creative Energy, into a phenomenal form perceptible to our limited senses.

The biblical statement *"Ye are gods"* does not apply to our Egos, but to the Potential welling within us. To repeat: it applies to the Potential generated by the individualization of the Universal Consciousness which, being omnipresent, must, *per force*, be also within us.

This and this alone is our true Self.

This and this alone is the "Divine Presence" welling within us. Only those that are 'called', *i.e.,* that recognize this Presence WITHIN themselves, can choose to be among the Few. This is the vital point.

We and we alone do the choosing.

This alone defines our Free Will. All else is subject to the indomitable Universal Laws.

And until we do, we remain the smart animals who do not recognize, let alone explore, their true, virtually infinite, potential.

Finally, a little quote from one of my favorite cosmologists, Carl Sagan:

"It is far better to grasp the universe as it really is than to persist in delusion, however satisfying and reassuring."

Like... grasping that the Big Bang happened out of nothing... like believing Universe continues to expand because of the ever swelling invisible 'black matter'... of 'black energy', like believing that that the phenomenal Universe is real and not a persistent delusion....?

Oh, ah... sorry.

These are the scientific theories that scientists consider real.

Except for the Few.

Like Einstein or Feynman, and a few others. So very few others...

~~~

(1) Quote from "*Romeo and Juliet*" by William Shakespeare.

PART THREE — FUTURE

*"To see a world in a grain of sand and heaven in a wild flower,
Hold infinity in the palm of your hand and eternity in an hour."*
William Blake (1757 - 1827)
English poet, painter, and printmaker.

"I make all things new."
Revelation 21:5 KJV

*"Instead of trying to cover the whole world with leather,
put on some sandals."*
Shantaideva (c. 685 - c. 763)
8th century Indian Buddhist scholar

Chapter 15
DOGMATIC MISUNDERSTANDING
(Fundamentalism in Religion and Science)

There is but a single difference between Science and Religion. Science is controlled exclusively by our mind, which is generated by our brain, creating self-reliance on Ego.

Religion is virtually the opposite. It is controlled almost exclusively by emotions. Also, although it accepts the existence of powers beyond those of our conscious mind (as generated by our biological computer), it invariably externalizes such a power, transferring it to some imaginary entity referred to as God. And this in spite of the assurance by Yeshûa's purported statement that:

HEAVEN IS WITHIN YOU
And
THE FATHER IS IN HEAVEN

To cut the story short, if we are to believe in Yeshûa's words (as Christians claim to do): The father is the Source of ALL creative power referred to as God. Hence:

The source of all power lies within you.

Yes. Within you and me. Within every single one of us. And the power is growing with our evolution.

We really are gods.

This, and this alone is the essence of Christ's teaching. Any other interpretation is a perversion by religious organizations which, by accepting this truth, would lose all authority, all power, and... all income.

And yet, by accepting Christ's teaching we inherit the power which he demonstrated while he walked this Earth. The power he demonstrated is within every single one of us. It is up to us to discover. And we could if we... *"had faith as small as a mustard seed"* (Matthew 17:20). That's all it would take. If you don't believe me, believe him. He, the Christ, was the only true atheist rejecting any and all authorities, powers, or influences outside his own being.

Of course, there would be consequences.

You'd no longer be able to blame anybody, not even God invented by religions, for the reality you've created.

You'd have to grow up.

Only please, once again, bear in mind that when I refer to 'you', I don't mean your body, your possessions, not even your Ego. After all, the first two are no more but illusion, and your Ego is your transient condition of Becoming. In fact, just the opposite. I mean you'd have to submit your will to the 'father', to the Creative Force within you. To your Higher Self.

It's not always easy. We all suffer from generations of mistaken conditioning that worships Egos, rather than teaching us humility and subservience to the Individualized Consciousness of the Creative Energy within us. But it can be done.

It was. By the FEW.

Our future is relatively simple. To repeat as the prophet once said, *"Ye are gods"*. How on earth could a prophet of old call us gods, when every priest, every preacher, every employee of a sacerdotal fraternity knows, without a shadow of doubt, that we, every one of us, is a sinner?

The old prophet, or... all those others, must be wrong. Surely gods are not sinners, are they?

Well?

You and you alone must decide which is right. Religionists must have found it a most inconvenient truth.[1]

We have a hint about our true nature from the book of invaluable knowledge—the book most of us refer to as the Bible. The book of unparalleled wisdom usurped by religionists and used for their own purposes.

The evangelists assure us that Yeshûa stated, quite firmly, that he and the 'father' are one. As all Christian religions consider that Yeshûa was the Son of God, we must assume that 'the father' was intended to be a designation for God. The fact that both, the Old and the New Testaments assure us that *"You are gods: you are all* (meaning us) *children of the Most High"* (Psalm 82:6 KJV), has been, and continues to be, studiously ignored.

It is much easier to control ignorant sinners than even "apprentice gods".

I apologize for repeating this statement, but it lies at the root of ALL misunderstanding created by religions. Intentionally or by accident, the statement was, and remains for them *a most inconvenient truth.*

Thus Yeshûa purportedly admitted the nobility of his heritage when admitting that: ***"I and the father are one"*** (John 10:30). And not *"the father and I are one"*. He insisted that neither Heaven nor the father (the progenitor of reality) exist outside his state of consciousness. Perhaps "Higher Consciousness", as in "Higher Self"? Perhaps he knew, even then that, as Einstein affirmed some two millennia later, that: *"**all else is an illusion**."*

He did not recognize the 'father' as an external entity commanding his becoming. He affirmed, quite adamantly, that all powers we seem to assign to a deity somewhere, up there, above the clouds, in some illusory Heaven, are, in fact, only... *within us*. Allow me to draw the conclusions:

The only reality is Consciousness.
In fact, we are states of Consciousness.
Indeed, all else is an illusion.

To sum up, I conclude that the immortal, indestructible, Consciousness of Being is not just within us but in fact *it is us*. We ARE this indestructible energy. It is you, and me. We are not the product of Egos, but the product of Self. Higher Self, if you will, or better still, every one of us is an:

INDIVIDUALIZATION
of the
OMNIPRESENT CONSCIOUSNESS.

Omnipresent, omniscient, indestructible, inexhaustible, eternal energy of... Consciousness.
The purpose of our Ego is but one. We are to translate the creative potential of all of the above into the phenomenal reality. Transient, ephemeral, illusory—yet the phenomenal reality in which we enjoy our Becoming. We are to create a mirror for the perfection that abides within us. We are to become *"as perfect as the father* (the potential) *is perfect."*[2]

If such be true, then we truly are gods. Or, at the very least, we are embodiments of the immortal and Creative Energy of Consciousness manifested through our minds. That is what we really are. *Gods*.

Ego, is quite another story. It is no more than a means of creating and appreciating the phenomenal illusion. And if I keep repeating this *ad nauseam*, you might, eventually believe me. And if not, you might believe Him. Although he did say: *"Why do ye not understand my speech?"*[3]

But that was 2,000 years ago. Perhaps we've grown up... a little, since?

(1) I am referring to the word '*sin*'. The mistranslation and misinterpretation of the Greek word *hamartia* is discussed in Chapter 2 above.

(2) "*Be ye therefore perfect, even as your Father which is in heaven is* perfect." (Matthew 5:48 KJV)

(3) John 8:43

Chapter 16.
GRATITUDE
(Where We Might Be)

> *"Entrepreneurs are simply those who understand that there is little difference between obstacle and opportunity and are able to turn both to their advantage."*
> **Niccolo Machiavelli (1469 - 15270)**
> A Florentine political philosopher,
> historian, musician, and poet.

> *"Gratitude unlocks the fullness of life. It turns what we have into enough, and more. It turns denial into acceptance, chaos to order, confusion to clarity.*
> *It can turn a meal into a feast, a house into a home, a stranger into a friend."*
> **Melody Beattie (1948 -)**
> Author

> *"E Pluribus Unum"*
> The traditional motto of the United States,
> suggested by the first Great Seal committee in 1776.

Judging by the stories about the Garden of Eden, we must have been created/born/evolved in Paradise, for the purpose of learning how to enrich our becoming towards our arrival in Heaven. Not the heaven of the Christians, nor the Moslem, but rather of the infinite number of realities referred to as *Devachan*[1] (see Chapter 2). Realities that we create in our consciousness. It is only through repeated reincarnations and prolonged examinations of the results of our efforts in the *Devachan* that we can make progress in our conversion of the Infinite Potential into Phenomenal Realities, which we can share with other individualized manifestations of the Omnipresent Consciousness. We must never forget that we are all *One*.

E Pluribus Unum.

Originally, in 1776, this motto of the United States, meaning *"Out of many, one"*, referred to the Union formed by a number of separate states. By now, surely, we can reach further. We can accept that all people, all citizens are united in the singularity of beliefs, of creative endeavour, and in enjoying the consequences of such.

If not, then the United States, like all empires before it, will fall by the wayside, and dissipate in the dusty volumes of history books. Yet, humanity, for now, will continue.

For a while?

Yet, there is a spanner in these works. The spanner is the Age of Aquarius. During this Age, as we know, the establishment of the few wielding power will fall. Those who oppose them will have no experience of guiding or ruling any group, let alone a country. The consequences are completely unpredictable. We can be sure of only one thing: the oncoming masses will have had no experience, opportunity, nor ability, to become as corrupt as the outgoing generation of our 'leaders'.

New kinds of leadership will emerge, and they will completely subvert the *status quo*. This is not necessarily a bad thing. Like with everything else, there will be a period of strife approaching anarchy, before the new elements, the new system, will become stabilized.

Few of us seem to realize that the acclaimed "democracy" has reached the point of no return. People do not rule, they never did. A system had been invented to make the masses, and even the *"Many that were called"* to think so. Yet, even in Greece, in the original cradle of democracy, only a few have ruled.

> For a long time, democracy in Athens was a sort of elitist political system, for only wealthy men (read: owners of properties) who had served in the military. Later on, the right of vote was extended to all Athenian men above the age of 20, which amounted to about 10 percent of the population. As such, slaves and women were never allowed a say in the matter.
> ...In fact, our modern democratic systems would be considered by Ancient Greeks as oligarchy, meaning, ruled by the few, as opposed to true democracy, which means "power, control by the people," or the many.[2]

Yes, we certainly live in a *sub rosa* oligarchy. Most billionaires didn't become billionaires by being democratic and in the US there are 607 of them. Fourteen of the world's richest 20 are from the US, mostly California and New York. Adding the multimillionaires to the list, collectively, the 2,153 people or families on the list are worth $8.7 trillion, which is quite a chunk of the $22.5 trillion national debt, which eventually *all* citizens must take part in dislodging.

So much for democracy.

It seems that the time is ripe for a change and, apparently, the Age of Aquarius will take care of that.

In the meantime, in the rest of the democratic world, not much has changed. While most people are now allowed to vote, their votes are manipulated or adapted to overriding considerations "for the good of the majority", or at the very least, for the good of the rich and famous.

Nevertheless, a change is coming. In some respects the present President of the USA is an integral part of it or, at least, of the so-called *Pluto Effect*.[3] He's certainly quite successful in destroying the st*atus quo*. And, after all, isn't that what real change requires?

Nevertheless, there is still a great deal we can be thankful for. It is only thanks to Eve, who symbolizes our subconscious, which in turn represents the memories, hence experiences, of our Ego from the day we became individualized entities of the Omnipresent Consciousness.

Yet, I do not recall ever reading, in the story of Eden, how grateful was either Adam or Eve for the lavishness of Paradise all around them. Perhaps, as Einstein would say, it was all an illusion? Or, as Yeshûa affirmed, it was all within them. Within their Consciousness.

For some of us, it still is.

Nevertheless, believe it or not, we can all revert to Eden by choosing to listen to the input from within rather than from without. Yes, we might all revert to living in Paradise again. All it really takes is... gratitude.

All animals are still becoming within Paradise. Nature provides for them, and sometimes we have the privilege to partake in the process. So why do we need gratitude? Because the alternatives are quite unpleasant. Because what we choose to see is what we get.

As we know, the Greeks called our Universe *Cosmos*, meaning "order, harmony" and even "ornament". And so it is, when looking at it with ***gratitude*** *and admiration*. But if we regard it with dispassionate, or even worse, with indifferent eyes, the picture changes.

The phenomenal Universe can be seen, and continue to be regarded, as a mess. It is best described by the word *chaos*. Not as in Greek *Theogony*, of some 700 BC, wherein

Chaos was preceded by Tartarus and followed by Gaia (Earth), but as a mess in need of intervention to set it in a more orderly fashion.[4]

We now know, (or pretend to know) that only life, which emerged from this primordial mess in different parts of its indescribable magnitude can wrench order out of chaos. What we observe in the night sky is a relative order that evolved over countless trillions (just billions according to our astrophysicists who tend to forget that the phenomenal Universe is eternal) of years. Yet, even now, we can witness galaxies smashing into each other, temporarily precluding further evolution. Not necessarily by what appears to be physical impact but by the havoc created by centripetal and centrifugal forces.

On the other hand, also as we know, all is energy, and energy cannot be destroyed. Gradually order will be restored; a state of relative balance will prevail; evolution will be given another chance, and some billions of years later intelligent life will emerge.

Isn't this what may have happened to us?

We may well be the products of such a history, although even locally, by phenomenal standards not so long ago, the asteroid belt may have happened after a collision of two planets within our local solar system.[5] We must hurry and grow in wisdom before another such event interrupts our evolution.

On the other hand, we do not have to worry.

Once again, as we already know, our real Selves consist of individualizations of energy that cannot be destroyed. We might lose our Egos, but will still have eternity to build them anew. And those Egos that survive will again enjoy their achievements in *Devachan*, or... be permanently recycled in Black Holes.

Isn't life fun?

> *How do you know but every bird*
> *that wings the airy way,*
> *Is an enormous world of delight,*
> *Closed to your senses five?*
>
> William Blake
> (1757 - 1827)

And this is where ORDER comes in. While diversity is unavoidable, as it is an indispensible ingredient of evolution, its excess is apt to produce chaos. As mentioned in Chapter 5 (*"Many are Called"*), there are only two forces that maintain relative order, and that is the centrifugal and centripetal energies. This is true on both the micro and the mega scale. Local disarrays can affect systems many light-years away. After all, the Universe is already beyond dimensional definitions, and yet it continues to expand.

This is a philosophical dilemma beyond our ability to comprehend. Yet, the phenomenal Universe will continue to expand to absorb continuous diversity.

And, once again, this is where we come in.

We can think, or imagine, that science will sate our curiosity, or that religion will deny the phenomenal reality. However, science can study only what is. Yet by the time we finish our examination, it, whatever it was, has metamorphosed into something else.

Good luck.

I tend to think that a million or two years from now, we, you and I, all of us, will change our minds. For now, there is only one solution to this dilemma:

Create your own Paradise and enjoy it.

The Bible and many other scriptural writings point our noses in the right direction. No, not into some sacerdotal societies who wish to exploit our ignorance. Now, as already mentioned, in the Age of Aquarius, we are all given a chance to grow up.

Some of us will continue to follow in the old Machiavellian footsteps. They'll continue to turn opportunities to their and only their advantage.

Like most politicians today?

Many others will continue to suspect that they are fooled, yet do little or nothing about it. Yet... this is the Age, in which the rest of us, the *"Third Party"*, can refuse to be fooled any longer. We can all stand on our own feet and listen to the silent voice within. This is the Age in which many of us can join the ranks of the Few.

For some the *silent voice within* is little more than a nagging thought they cannot get rid off. For others, it is the source of all inspiration. All artists, writers, and composers would produce nothing or, at the very least, nothing original, were they unable to listen to the silent voice within. Once heard, they convert it and often develop it to allow others to hear it. Or, in case of painters or sculptors, to see it. And in some cases, to appreciate it with other senses, such as our appreciation of poetry. The inner voice is our immortal Self asserting Its presence within us.

A mere whisper can become an immortal work of art!

Many people seem unaware of this. They seem unaware that within them there is an inexhaustible well of ideas, all begging to be heard, acknowledged, and then converted into the phenomenal reality. We are all artists, all are creators; yet most of us do not seem to be aware of the potential within us.

I am neither a teacher nor a preacher, but I do have a presumptuous request.

Listen. Always listen, and you will be richly rewarded. After all, the voice comes from an infinite Source!

Aren't we lucky?

Let us return to Eden. In the Garden of Eden we can grow the Consciousness of *gratitude*. We can restore the balance and gratitude for the gifts bestowed on us. Imagine the miracle of our phenomenal bodies. Billions of cells, trillions of microorganisms, all functioning, for the most part, in perfect order and harmony. And then the plethora of other miracles that surround us. All grateful hearts will find them. As for the others...?

There are some Egos that refuse to be grateful.
Usually they are the blind — leading the blind.

And then we can try, as best we can, to contribute to the Universe. If history repeats itself, then even if the whole of the "Third Party", let alone all who had already been "Called", who had already been given a chance to do their absolute best, most probably only a Few will make it. Only a Few will listen to that voice within.

To listen to the inner voice we must silence our Egos.

The consolation is that regardless of the input from all who do not make the grade, their contribution might well add to the diversity of the Universe, without actually enhancing it. Enhancement may come later. Thus, no one should give up hope. We are all integral parts, hence "instruments of the Universe", and all we need do is our best. The Universe will take care of the rest.

In *DELUSIONS* I asked "Where we Might Be". Now we know the answer. *Wherever we want to be.* After all, reality is what we make it. It is, and always has been, up to us. I opted for the return to Eden. I think I already have. I can't imagine being more blessed than I already am. Even in *Devachan*.

Once again, good luck.

~~~

(1) I strongly suspect that the *Olympus* created by the ancient Greeks bears a strong resemblance to the *Devachan*.

(2) "Things You May Not Know About Democracy in Ancient Greece" https://theculturetrip.com/europe/greece/articles/7-things-you-may-not-know-about-democracy-in-ancient-greece/

(3) A term I borrowed from my novel *AWAKENING—The Pluto Effect*. Originally this terms was derived from astrological predictions.

(4) *Tartarus* is one of the realms within Hades. The Underworld and it's entirety is within Hades and ruled by its namesake the god also known to the Romans as Pluto. Within Hades the Greeks and Romans believed there were several plains not too dissimilar to Dante's *Inferno* (Wikipedia). I suspect that already then they suspected that the expression "several plains" is equivalent to several states of consciousness.

(5) Half of Mars is flat, the other side mountainous. Any suggestions? (Immanuel Velikovsky explores this possibility in his books.)

Chapter 17
WE REALLY ARE GODS
(What We Might Be)

> *"I am a magnificent human being.
> I am without equal in all of creation.
> My mind and body are so magnificently constructed
> that no feat of engineering could ever duplicate
> the uniqueness in myself. I will transcend all ordinary thinking and
> dwell entirely in my higher self."*
> **Evelyn M. Monahan**
> Author of:
> *The Miracle of Metaphysical Healing*

> *"A child-like man is not a man whose development has been
> arrested; on the contrary, he is a man who has given himself
> a chance of continuing to develop long after most adults have
> muffled themselves in the cocoon
> of middle-aged habit and convention."*
> **Aldous Leonard Huxley, (1894 - 1963)**
> British author

> *"Ye are gods;
> and all of you are children of the most High."*
> **Psalm 82:6 (KJV)**

In *DELUSIONS*, this chapter ends with another question: *"So, once again, who are we?"* The title later transposed to "*What we might be*". It deals with the future.

The answer is relatively simple.

Once again, we are individualizations of the Omnipresent Consciousness and we might, eventually, become aware of it. What is our purpose that's quite another story. In the East they call is *dharma*. Every single one of us is entrusted with an individual, unique purpose. As time (other than in the phenomenal reality) does not exist, there is no hurry for us to fulfill our destiny. When we do, we are likely to lose our personality and merge, once again, with the infinite ocean of the Omnipresent Consciousness.

Or, we might be assigned another ennobling task. Such seems to be the privilege of *Bodhisattvas*.[1] They remain in the phenomenal reality for the sake of others.

Eventually, in the fullness of the 'nonexistent' time, i.e. when the assigned tasks in the present phenomenal Universe have been met, we might be individualized again, to expand the phenomenal Universe even further towards Infinity.

So what is our purpose?

There are three reasons for our presence in the phenomenal Universe:

(1) to sustain it;
(2) to enhance it;
(3) to expand it.

It seems that, as always, a trinity enters our lives. To sustain it is relatively easy. That's what nature does, and we are parts of nature.

Eventually, after millions of phenomenal years, we may reach the conscious level of some gods proliferating our many myths. What it really means is that we shall finally learn how to manipulate energy and to metamorphose it into different elements of the physical, hence illusory reality. Such power could vastly exceed the limited powers wielded by the gods of our many myths.

The Greeks alone give accounts of many gods: Zeus, Hera, Aphrodite, Apollo, Ares, Artemis, Athena, Demeter, Dionysus, Hephaestus, Hermes, and Poseidon, to mention just a few. And there are many other myths that enhance our past, that could hardly all be the results of our, immature imaginations. On the other hand, if we reached back another few billion years, we might have met gods whose existence is long forgotten, yet who might have created the reality of the Universe which we now recognize as real. Yet gods that have long achieved immortality beyond our ability to perceive them.

Real—at least until Einstein called it, yes, the whole Universe, an illusion. Were the gods also an illusion, even as our physical bodies are? And yet, the energies that created our reality must, *perforce*, be indestructible.

It seems that J.B.S. Haldane must have been right. *"The universe is not only stranger than we imagine, it is stranger than we can imagine."* Was this also true of the gods of our past?

On the other hand, let us never forget that the only true reality is the *Omnipresent Consciousness*. Hence, as implied above, manipulating the rates of vibration of energies is, and always will remain, the manipulation of illusions.

We have Albert Einstein to thank for this.

Evelyn Monahan's philosophy seems to imply that we already are gods. Or, at the very least, might be. Might become. Some ancient prophets, eastern yogis, gurus or a few enlightened people, might agree with her. According to Christianity, we're all just sinners.

And yet Yeshûa has said that the Creative Energy (the father) is in Heaven, and Heaven is within us. That each one of us could wield that power, that Creative Energy, if we had *"faith as small* as *a mustard seed"*— that with even that little faith we could move mountains.[2]

Was he wrong?

On the other hand, to repeat yet again, beyond the phenomenal reality there is no time. Within the eternity of the Universe we already *are* every bit the statement Mpnahan made about us. And, it just so happened, that in her own life she'd proven that she spoke from personal experience.

At the age of 22 she was involved in an accident which left her blind. She faced the prospect of living the rest of her life in darkness. Her head injury had also resulted in 12 epileptic seizures a day. Medicine reduced them to 10, but it did nothing for her blindness.

But her tribulations weren't over.

Four years later she was involved in another car accident which, in addition to her previous injuries that were beyond the expertise of the medical profession to do anything about, she now added a paralysis in her right arm.

She was blind, epileptic and disabled for nine years.

After nine years of trying all that the medical profession had to offer without any effect, she decided to take matters into her own hands. One hand... the other one was paralyzed. She began her research into metaphysical healing.

Within ten days of trying her metaphysical techniques, she regained her eyesight. The epileptic seizures left her at the same time. Her physician confirmed that there was no sign of epilepsy. A week later her right arm lost its paralysis. The medical profession offered no explanation.

She was, indeed, a magnificent human being.

There is almost a paradoxical consequence to this story. Had the physicians been able to help her, none of this would have happened. It is only their ineptness that drove her to discover the magnificent powers within herself.

The Miracle of Metaphysical Healing *would have remained unknown. Even now, only the FEW have heard about it. ,*

What concerns the rest of us is not only that the medical profession couldn't help her but that she followed exactly the instructions given us some 2,000 years ago by a man whom, to this day, many worship as God. Yeshûa, known later as Jesus, did state that whatsoever we ask the *"father in my (his) name"* will be given us. In biblical symbolism, 'name' implies nature. Adam named all the animals in the Garden of Eden, and thus defined their nature, remember?

To eliminate the symbolic mumbo-jumbo, Yeshûa appears to have said that whosoever addresses the Creative Power within himself or herself in the name of their Higher Self, his/her wish will be granted. He, Yeshûa, also confirmed the ancient prophet's assurance that *"we are gods."* Hence, the power rests within us. Within the immortal Self that dwells in our immortal Consciousness. All we need is faith grater than... *"a grain of mustard seed."*

Doesn't sound so hard, does it?

Yet, not many followed Monahan's let alone Yeshûa's example.

And yet they were, and continue to be, ill-advised not to have done so. Medical ineptness began some centuries ago. There are many stories of medical professionals who, in spite of the Hippocratic oath, seemingly specialized in hurting if not killing their patients.

By far the worst examples are the thousands who were butchered by lobotomy. It started early, around 1880s, when a Swiss 'physician' by the name Gottlieb Burckhardt removed a portion of a woman's brain, converting her from *"a dangerous and demented person into a quiet demented woman."*

This I read in Bill Bryson's book *The Body*.[4]

Later, Mr. Bryson continues, the 'neurosurgeon' tried the process on five more patients, succeeding in killing three of them, while the other two developed epilepsy. For now, surprisingly, he stopped.

However, five decades later, a professor of neurology at

the University of Lisbon, Egas Moniz, discarded all scientific procedures. Apparently, without any research, he proceeded to operate under lamentable conditions, supervising his inept assistants to perform countless removals of portions of frontal lobes. In spite of his barbaric standards of hygiene he was awarded, as recently as 1949 a Nobel Prize in Physiology or Medicine. They didn't say which. They probably didn't care, as long as he killed people?

And, writes Bill Bryson, it didn't stop there.

In the United States, where they hate to be second best in anything, a 'doctor' named Walter Jackson Freeman, became Moniz's fervent acolyte performing lobotomies for the next 40 years. It must have been an exciting hobby as on one particular tour he is said to have lobotomized 225 people in twelve days.

> *"He inserted a standard household ice pick into the brain through the eye socket, tapping it through the skull bone with a hammer, then wriggled it vigorously to sever neural connections."*

Mr. Bryson quotes Freeman's actual description of his procedures in practically the same words. Yet, by some miracle, Freeman and his assistants apparently managed to avoid jail although it became evident that Freeman and others like him left a trail of human wreckage behind them.

One can but wonder what Evelyn Monahan would have to say. Apparetnly she was lucky enough to evade the talons of medicine for nine years. Probably this fact alone kept her alive.

Don't misunderstand me. Within the medical profession there are also the Few, the Many, and regrettably the Third Party, of which a few examples are given above. Speaking for myself, I wish to thank Evelyn for opening our eyes.

There may be a simple reason for all of the above. People attempt to affect 'miracles' by changing the phenomenal reality. This is not how her system works. What we must do, instead, is to substitute a perfect condition for the imperfect one that has been created by our Ego. To do so, we must reach out beyond the phenomenal reality. It seems that the only way to make contact with the power welling within us is through the "straight and narrow", which is the narrow passage to the pineal gland. To reach this gland with our thoughts we must dismiss awareness of the artificial awareness of Ego, of that which ties us to the phenomenal world.

A state of deep relaxation is a *sine qua non* to affect the seemingly miraculous changes in the phenomenal reality, which, as we know, is a "persistent illusion". The pineal gland is activated by the alpha waves of our brain.

This, according to Evelyn Monahan, energizes the Mind. *The mind, not the brain.* Remember Max Planck? He said that *"This mind is the matrix of all matter."* Max Planck was not a religious preacher. He was a top-flight physicist. After all, they don't give Nobel Prizes for Physics to just anybody.

(Physics in not medicine.)

And now, Evelyn Monahan takes our mind to the next stage of awareness. She defines her healings as miraculous. We ought to note that miracles are not creations of 'things'. They are creations of *reality*. Some might say, they are creations of illusions we perceive as real. At least, I suspect, Albert Einstein would think so.

Does it matter?

Also, please note, that we do not energize our mind through relaxation—which is, nevertheless, a prerequisite for success, but by the energy of alpha waves generated by the pineal gland. Luckily, this happens automatically once a sufficient state of relaxation has been reached.

Remember Einstein: **ALL IS ENERGY.**

And now I shall attempt to explain my statement above that *Miracles are not creations of things but are creations of new reality.*

Whether we call them *Newton's Laws, Universal Laws, Thoughts of God,* or by any other name, nature conforms to certain rules.

No one can deny or contradict any Law that controls any reality. I say 'any', as there is an endless number of realities, virtually a different for every human being. Many, almost all of us, choose to accept an objective reality dismissing our subjective concepts of it. As for the reality which we experienced having been given 'skins' (Genesis 3:21) the rules apply to all of us equally. In the Bible, the 'skins' represent our first awareness of the illusion of our physical bodies—in fact, of the physical, illusory reality (*vide* Einstein again). We can only speculate that before this evolutionary event we had been disembodied individualized states of the energy of Consciousness.

(Think of the bodies we carry in our dreams.)

And, we are told, until this reality has served its purpose, not "one iota" (Matthew 5:18) can be changed in it. The Universal Laws of **every** reality are fixed. We cannot change the reality but **we can change our illusion** of it.

After all, phenomenal reality is but an illusion.

So, how can we contradict the Laws by performing miracles?

We can't.

Miracles cannot and do not contradict the Universal Laws controlling a particular (objective) reality. What miracles do is to transfer the recipient of the reality to a higher level (reality created by higher rate of vibration of energy), and then transport the results "ready-made" to his or

CONCLUSIONS 161

her previous illusion.

We do something akin to what happens in our dreams, where we perform the seemingly impossible. Yet, it has been reported, that exercises performed, particularly in *lucid* dreams, carry the results or consequences to the waking reality. To repeat:

**ALL
realities are phenomenal illusions.**

The difference is that with 'miracles' we awaken into an illusion of reality which for us has changed to incorporate the result of the miracle. The miracle is not the change created in the phenomenal reality but in our perception of the new reality. All realities are co-extant within us, but we are capable of experiencing them only one at a time. Nevertheless, a change in our perception is reflected in the phenomenal reality.

All realities are created by our thoughts and emotions, and the results are experienced by our sensual perceptions. Hence, the illusion changes.

Let us return once more to healing. Metaphysical healing. If we accept Einstein's conclusion that all is illusion, that the world we live in is no more than the product, or 'outpicturing', of our Consciousness, of our imagination, then our attitude towards healing must change. We shall learn that the process of healing does not change our illusory body (which doesn't really exist), but it changes the illusion of the body we inhabit. What we must do is to make sure, to quote Einstein again, that we create a "persistent illusion." Isn't it a question of faith?

We must change the nature of the illusion.

Hence, we are gods.

Whatever we imagine with our (what Monahan calls) "energized mind", will become, or can become, our new reality. And, for as long as we believe that it is real, it will remain real—as real as the rest of the Universe which we imagine is all around us.

What fascinates me is that so many people manage to imagine virtually the same reality. This makes the reality persistent. It sounds miraculous until we realize that we are all One. That until we individualize any aspects of it, we all experience the same reality in which others live.

Perhaps that's why there are only the *Few*.

The *Few* who believe that they are gods. That Heaven is within them. That the creative power which created that Heaven also abides within them. That the creator is their own Higher Self. And the energy used to access this Heaven is our energized mind. Not the mind generated by our brain, but by the mind which created the illusion of our brain, which generates the artificial reality.

All we need do is to forsake our Egos, forsake that which keeps us apart, and the rest comes naturally. All we need is *"faith no bigger than a mustard seed..."*[2] Remember?

That's all.

The rest is history. To repeat, the Bible has **nothing** to do with religion. Hence, we can put a new twist on the expression above... *the rest is our future.*

And finally there are
SOME NEW DISCOVERIES.

First, let us make sure we are talking about the same thing. I want to discuss neurons.

> A **neuron**, or **nerve cell**, is an electrically excitable cell that communicates with other cells via specialized connections called synapses. It is the main component of nervous tissue. All animals except sponges and placozoans have neurons, but other multicellular organisms such as plants do not.
>
> (Wikipedia - Neuron)

To get to the newest discoveries, we must understand the structure of a neuron. In fact of some 100 billion of them hiding in our heads. The neurons have specialized projections called *dendrites* and *axons*. Dendrites bring information into the cell body, while axons extract information to share with other neurons through tiny gaps between neurons known as *synapses*.

So far, so good...

But now our scientists discovered that our neurons not only communicate with each other through electrochemical impulses across the synapses, (as reported in Chapter 1), but that at the 'end' of each individual neuron the tree-like protoplasmic extensions of nerve cells known as *dendrites* propagate electrochemical stimulations capable of solving computational problems without involving other neurons.

Surprised? Well there is still more!

The neurons, with *dendrites* which have executive power to act creatively on their own, are capable of producing photons of light, we've come to know as *biophotons*. More about them later.

And this leads us to solving another mystery that was ignored for thousands of years. Have you noticed that everything that our scientists cannot understand they invariably dismissed as fantasy, superstition, or as non-existent, while simultaneously it is usually accepted by our religionists as miracles?

Well, as I've pointed out in *DELUSIONS*, all too often, they are both wrong.

And now we come to the crux of the matter.

The Science and Technology Newsletter reports that the halos of saints might be the real thing. Apparently from ancient Greece and Rome, as well as in the teachings of Hinduism, Buddhism, and Islam, people regarded as sacred had been depicted with shining, circular glow around their heads. They also adorn the heads on all ecclesiastic paintings.

While such images were respectfully accepted by the 'faithful', to my knowledge (and I had been a Catholic for many years) nobody ever questioned the reason for this luminous halo. To my knowledge, the faithful, still don't.

As always, we need reminding that we are still in an evolutionary kindergarten.

The halos around the heads of some very exceptional people appear to be formed by *bona fide* photons.

To repeat, our scientists now claim that neurons in mammalian brains are capable of producing photons of light. Strangely enough, these "*biophotons*" are in the spectrum of visible light, from near-infrared to violet. This might not only be responsible for the auras appearing around the heads of some advanced people, but lead the scientists to suspect that our neurons might be able to communicate through light.

The next step will be to discover if the biophotons might be connected to the energy of our Consciousness.

And... once again, there is more...

The biophotons emitted by our brains might well be affected by *quantum entanglement*.[3] Apparently, a human brain could convey more than a billion biophotons per second. This, in turn, suggests that if we could communicate with biophotons, the more light we produce, the greater would be our communication with each other.

And then there is the quantum entanglement.

If such were to apply, if there is a strong link between these photons, we could communicate with each other across immeasurable distances. The metaphysical inspirations which heretofore belonged only in the realm of religions, would suddenly enter the skeptic's conceptualization of our reality.

The next step is to discover what, if any, is the relationship between light and Consciousness. According to the late Paul Twitchell, the creator of what has since his death became the religion of Eckankar, (which he swore would never happen) our reality consists of *light and sound*. He might have been closer to the truth than his detractors gave him credit.

Whatever your or my interpretation of reality, we seem to be drifting closer and closer to what was once referred to as Spirit. I consider Its Energy to be synonymous with Consciousness. Yet whatever level of understanding our scientists have reached, there seems to be a lot more to *light* than we are, at present, aware of.

At the risk of boring you, I'll repeat that we are still in the kindergarten of knowledge. We have barely scraped the surface. Hence, wherever the latest experiments take us, there is always more that remains unknown. The Energy of Consciousness can metamorphose in countless, probably infinite, numbers of ways. And we, the people, have the potential of increasing that number.

Philosopher Philip Goff, associate professor in philosophy at Central European University in Budapest, answering questions about "panpsychism", (mentioned in Chapter 9), appears to agree with my assumptions. Panpsychism, for those to whom this is still a new concept, is the doctrine, or belief, that everything material, however small, has an element of individual Consciousness. Or, to put it in my own words, it means that all is Energy, and the prime Energy of all is Consciousness. In my reasoning, this approach unites philosophy with science or, at least, I suspect it would, in Albert Einstein's eyes.

Who is to tell us that electrons and quarks do not experience Consciousness? If they don't, then how do they know how to act, how to behave, how to retain their essential nature, within the environment of energies continuously bombarding them from all directions? How do they know how to 'be' electrons or quarks?

After all, all is energy, remember?

I suspect that *Rupert Sheldrake PhD,* (often referred to as a renegade British biologist), best known for his hypothesis of *morphic resonance,* which argues that telepathy and other paranormal abilities are inherent in all nature. Even if most of us cannot use them... as yet.

We are immortal, remember?

Furthermore...

> *Sheldrake's morphic resonance posits that "memory is inherent in nature" and that "natural systems... inherit a collective memory from all previous things of their kind." Sheldrake proposes that it is also responsible for "telepathy-type interconnections between organisms." His advocacy of the idea offers idiosyncratic explanations of standard subjects in biology such as development, inheritance, and memory.*
> (Rupert Sheldrake - WIKIPEDIA)

This proposal assured the maintenance of diversity, which seems to be the prerequisite of all evolution (not to mention the continuous expansion of the phenomenal Universe)

My comment of Dr. Sheldrake's theory is simply, "when you're right, you're right." His postulates explain how nature works without any contradictions derived from any observations. Nevertheless, *morphic resonance* in not accepted by the "scientific community". Perhaps they need a few more centuries to catch up with the Few.

And then there is another, perhaps the most exciting implication of the proposal, or should one say theory, that brain produces light waves. The most direct consequence of such an idea would be that our Consciousness might not be contained within our bodies. Or, at least, not only within our bodies. That the **I AM** is as much within and without the reality we occupy within the physical, *i.e.*, phenomenal environment.

That we are more than flesh and bones.

Those experimenting with *Quantum entanglement*, have suggested that the quantum action may be 100,000 times faster than light. With all the due respects to our scientists, this is impossible. The reason quantum action appear to be simultaneous is because it is. Only, it *doesn't* travel in any particular direction, no matter how absurd the speed.

It is already there.

Sooner or later we must accept the concept of the *Omnipresence* of the basic, initial, or embryonic energy we know as *Consciousness*. It, and only IT, is omnipresent. It also already possesses all possible manifestations in their potential form. Whatever happens to one or two or more elements which display the same resonance, *i.e.,* which vibrate at the same, identical rate, which are in harmony—in other words which manifest in the phenomenal reality in synchronicity—must happen to all the others.

This is the mystery of our individualization of the

Energy of Consciousness. While it is individualized, it remains inseparable from its Source. In fact, they remain One, even as every drop in the ocean is integral to that ocean; only Consciousness is omnipresent, while the ocean isn't. Yet every single drop retains all the characteristics of the entire ocean, (barring... pollution?)

But one of the most exciting implications of the discovery that our brains can produce light is that it suggests that our Consciousness (or spirit) is not contained within our bodies. This implication is completely overlooked by scientists.

As discussed, *Quantum entanglement* states that two entangled photons react simultaneously. If one of the photons is affected, the other photon, no matter where the other photon is in the Universe, is likewise affected without any delay.

It has been suggested that, maybe there is a world that exists within light. In such a reality, no matter where you are in the Universe, photons would act as portals that enable communication between different locations, even if such were light-years away from each other.

Maybe our spirit and/or Consciousness communicates with our bodies through these biophotons. And the more light we produce, the more we awaken and embody the wholeness of our Consciousness.

This would explain the phenomenon of why the state of a photon is affected simply by being observed, as it has been proven in many quantum experiments.

It seems that our observation communicates something through our biophotons to the photon that is being observed, in a fashion similar to *quantum entanglement*. It might be that light, like Consciousness, is just one unified substance that is scattered throughout our Universe and affected by each light particle.

I do not lose hope that in one or two million years we shall solve, or confirm, such 'suspicions' and make conscious use of them. Obviously, our perception of reality will change beyond recognition. At the moment, nothing of this is even close to being a theory. But, as Einstein had said,

> "The important thing is to not stop questioning.
> **Curiosity**
> has its own reason for existing."

It also seems that only asking questions that verge on metaphysical can bring us closer to the mysteries of the *"thoughts of God"*. After all, Aristotle, Plato, Immanuel Kant, René Descartes, David Hume, Ludwig Wittgenstein, Baruch Spinoza, Thomas Aquinas, Martin Heidegger, Friedrich Nietzsche, Bertrand Russell, Arthur Schopenhauer, and a host, yes, *a host of others*, cannot be all wrong!

I strongly suspect, though, that most of today's scientists AND adherents to established religions would think so. Yet, in spite of the scientific establishment which protects their theories, without daring to reach out into the unknown, without reaching out to grasp photons proliferating our phenomenal Universe, there will always be those who dare.

All mysteries hide within the light.

Who knows? Perhaps the time will come when halos radiating from our heads with multihued biophotons will adorn most of our heads. As the frequency of our vibrations rises, so will our enlightenment. Even the word

enLIGHTenment

points the way towards a union of light and Consciousness. An Indian guru, recognized by many as a great mystic, once said: *"I sit in the light, I am the light, the **light** is me."* They still worship him in India.

Another man that to this day many recognize as God, once said, *"I am the **light** of the world."*(5)

And he was. Still is.

You too, might be, if you see the light.

~~~

(1) In Mahayana Buddhism *bodhisattvas* is a person who is able to reach nirvana but delays doing so out of compassion in order to save suffering beings. (Wikipedia)

(2) Matthew 17:20, Luke 17:6 (KJV)

(3) Quantum entanglement - *Science Daily* states: *"Quantum entanglement* is a *quantum* mechanical phenomenon in which the *quantum* states of two or more objects have to be described with reference to each other, even though the individual objects may be spatially separated." Although the effect passed an increasing number of tests, Einstein call it "spooky action at a distance."

(4) Bill Bryson, *The Body* (Doubleday Canada)

(5) John 8:12 (KJV)

Chapter 18
PHENOMENAL DIFFUSION
(The God Diffusion)

> *"Knowing there is an Unknown that cannot be known is the dawn of wisdom."*
> **Wu Hsin**
> The Lost Writings.
> (Possibly Roy Melvyn. His pen-name means: "no mind")

> *"There is nothing more difficult to take in hand, more perilous to conduct, or more uncertain in its success, than to take the lead in the introduction of a new order of things."*
> **Niccolò Machiavelli (1469 - 1527)**
> Florentine political philosopher, historian, musician, and poet.

> *"The world is full of magical things patiently waiting for our wits to grow sharper".*
> **Bertrand Russell (1872 - 1970)**
> British philosopher

It has been said of John Haldane's statement that *"the world is stranger than we can imagine"* was the most satisfying story of the 20th century. Perhaps because all physical theories deal with the phenomenal reality which, again according to Einstein, does not really exist.

As pointed out already, it is but an illusion.

Hence we are forced to return to metaphysics to make sense out of the reality in which we enjoy our becoming. We live in a reality in which the energies are at different rates of vibration, are in constant ferment, fluctuation, and permanent metamorphosis.

Our Individualized "units of" Consciousness are the

only energy which points the way to our ongoing Becoming. It is vital to appreciate that the energy of the Individualized Consciousness is characterized by the identical, *i.e.,* infinite, rate of vibrations as the Omnipresent Consciousness. It is also indivisible from Its Source.

I spell it with capital letters, to emphasize Its Infinite Potential. The phenomenal reality, no matter how transient, neither would nor could exist without It. It is the eternal Source of all phenomenal manifestations. It has the attribute of being able to metamorphose into any other energy of slower vibrations.

As the Potential is Infinite, so must, *perforce*, be the phenomenal reality which gives us awareness of the Potential.

Furthermore, as the omnipresence of the infinite rate of vibrations of the Energy of Consciousness precludes the existence of time, all possible potential versions of you and me, and everyone else, already exist, although we are only aware of the one embodiment upon which we place our attention. (In the philosophical sense, this might be the extension of the Quantum Field Theory.)

This is, inter alia, how strange our Universe is.

What we appear to have problems accepting is that the Universal Consciousness is not a product of AI. Or that being omnipresent, It permeates all of Its phenomenal creation. Yet, every cell in your and my body knows its place, its function, and its purpose.

And this does not apply just to us, humans.

This Universal Consciousness permeates ALL of Its phenomenal creation. It is the essence of all flora and fauna. Of every animal, every bird, fish, of every tree, and every blade of grass. Of every atom and subatomic particle. Of every wave of every energy that makes up the Universe in which we find our Becoming.

Of all energies of lower rates of vibration.

We shall accept this only if we agree that Universal Consciousness is the Creative Energy of the whole Universe. Of all phenomenal realities. That the phenomenal Universe, no matter how transient, is the expression of Energy which the religious people call God.

The phenomenal world is God's diffusion.
All of it.
The diffusion of the Creative Consciousness.

What I am about to share with you is valid only for those who accept that the Bible is a compendium of knowledge and has *nothing whatever to do with any religion*. It always was such, until religionists usurped it to control people's minds, behaviour, as well as for the financial benefits. You'll notice that the rest of the phenomenal world, of nature, does not suffer from such an illusion.

There is a single sentence in the Bible which gives us the scientific explanation of reality. To understand it we need to accept the following truth:

1. The nature of the Universe consists of a duality, of potential and phenomenal, *i.e.,* of a physical reality, characterized by Being and Becoming.

2. Being is the permanent condition which exists outside the parameters of the phenomenal Universe, *i.e,* beyond restrictions of time or space.

3. Being incorporates all possible modes of Becoming. All that ever was, is, or could be, already exists in its potential form.

4. Becoming is a system of gradual translation of the Potential into the energies of phenomenal realities. The complexity of this process results in 'life' and the eventual

evolution of artificial intelligence.

6. Phenomenal reality consists only of energy at different rates of vibration.

When we restore the unity of the energies of Being and Becoming into the Singularity of Consciousness (*i.e.,* unify the Ego generated by AI with the Individualized Consciousness within us) we shall be able to repeat Yeshûa's admonition in the sentence:

"I AND MY FATHER ARE ONE."

Please note: not "my Father and I", but "I and my Father". The order in which the 'factors' are placed is of vital importance to accept this dualistic concept. *I AM* is both, that which I was, that which I am, and that which I could ever be. It also means that *I AM* is pure Energy of Consciousness.

Consequently, that which I have become in this fragment of phenomenal time, and that which I ever could be, are *One*. Hence, Being and Becoming are also *One*. What changes our awareness is that upon which we place our attention. Of course, we cannot place our attention on that of which we are not (as yet) aware. Hence the necessity of enlightenment.

This sentiment, or fact, is further explained by the statement that Heaven (the potential energy of reality of everything), and the Father (the nature of what I am and what I ever could be), *are one and the same*. Hence the two are ONE.

There is one more secret that has been unveiled in the Bible, and that appears to be misunderstood by religionists. The so-called *"Lord's Prayer"*, better known as *"Our Father..."* explains the last mystery. This is explained by a single word,

"OUR"

Hence the 'Father', or the Creative Energy within you and me, are ONE. We are ALL expressions of the same Energy of Consciousness. The nature of the Energy of Being within you and within me is the same. The same Creative Consciousness.

There is only One Source that manifests in the phenomenal reality through countless—probably a near-infinite—number of phenomenal entities, representing infinite possibilities, by contributing to the ever-increasing diversity of the ever-expanding Universe.

Welcome to my reality!

Or as John Haldane would say, welcome to a world that is *Stranger Than We Can Imagine...*

Chapter 19
THE NEW DAWN
(The Beginning of the End)

> *A democracy which makes or even effectively prepares for modern, scientific war must necessarily cease to be democratic. No country can be really well prepared for modern war unless it is governed by a tyrant, at the head of a highly trained and perfectly obedient bureaucracy.*
> **Aldous Leonard Huxley, (1894 - 1963)**
> British author

> *"United States is unusual among the industrial democracies in the rigidity of the system of ideological control - 'indoctrination', we might say - exercised through the mass media."*
> **Noam Chomsky (1928 -)**
> American linguist, philosopher, cognitive scientist

> *"It has been said that democracy is the worst form of government except for all the others that have been tried."*
> **Sir Winston Churchill (1874 - 1965)**
> British politician, prime minister, and writer.

It is always darkest just before Dawn. Some of us need traumatic experiences to shake us free from generations of tradition. Others reach their conclusions through mental acrobatics. A few indulge in daily contemplation, which consists of listening to the silent voice within. Still others benefit from the Buddhist way. Without any apparent effort, they awaken as though emerging from a deep sleep. Yet most regard the phenomenal reality as the only reality, hoping that somewhere, "up there" there is a heaven where they'll spend eternity resting in peace. The last group, regrettably the vast majority, are the followers of religions.

My parents took their religious conditioning to their

grave. Jimmy Carter, the son of a Southern Baptist Sunday schoolteacher, awakened in the nick of time. At the age of 76, he said:

> *"I became a Southern Baptist when I was 11 years old. My father was a Southern Baptist before me and so was my grandfather..."*

The former President has said that the Southern Baptist Convention violated the basic premises of his Christian faith, such as prohibiting women from being pastors and telling wives to be submissive to their husbands. It couldn't have been easy to break with t the radition of three generations. Perhaps the former President was aware that the early Christian Church enjoyed many women bishops who ran their congregations. He might have wondered whether Christianity was moving forward, or regressing...

Then, though still in the early days of Christianity, men usurped power. Power that demanded obedience under the threat of Hell.

The misogynistic approach probably started with the mandatory celibacy. Some claim it only began in the 11th century, but most date it back to St. Leo the Great, a 5th century pope, as the time when celibacy was accepted in the West. This measure assured that the Church inherited their priests' possessions, rather than their sons or family.

The rest is history.

I found my freedom much sooner.

I concluded that the Jesuits who attempted to instill religion in my youthful subconscious violated the laws of nature. They seemed to have claimed that sex was a sin. They asked me to promise never to attempt to "get lucky" again. They did this at the Confessional. Hence, they left me no choice.

I was, then, in my late teens.

However, it took me another 20 years to discover spirituality. A very different cup of tea from religion. Religions tend to usurp your freedom; spirituality invariably sets you free. In fact, it offers incredible freedom, the freedom only immortality can offer. And Heaven. Here and now.

The Age of Aquarius offers this freedom to us all.

Yet, it is always darkest just before Dawn. The Age of Aquarius is preceded by the *Pluto Effect*, which eradicates as many errors invading our previous consciousness as possible, without breaking the Universal Laws. The purpose of this purge is to make room for new ideas.

> [It may be of interest to you that I've written a number of novels that illustrate this condition. Book Two of my Aquarius Trilogy is entitled *PLUTO EFFECT*. You'll find it, and all my books, fiction and non-fiction, on Amazon and other distributors, under my pen name Stan I.S. Law. Enjoy!] [1]

The beginning of the end (mentioned in *DELUSIONS*) is when we begin to question the substance of our reality. Einstein went through the process late in life, and his conclusions have erased all presumptions of science and religions up to now. Other great thinkers went through the same process two millennia ago.

A Chinese philosopher Chuang Tzu (399 - 295 BC), popularly known as Zhuangzie, also faced the problem of recognizing reality:

> *"I dreamed I was a butterfly, flitting around in the sky; then I awoke. Now I wonder: Am I a man who dreamt of being a butterfly, or am I a butterfly*

dreaming that I am a man?"

Is life just an illusion?

It certainly is transient. Compared to the rest of the phenomenal Universe, it is fleeting, ephemeral. But, the question remains, is it real?

For many, this is how it starts. We begin to question our ability to trust the evidence provided by our senses. Then, gradually, we begin to question the very nature of all our perceptions.

Finally, we become aware of being more than we heretofore thought we were. The infinite creative potential that dwells within our consciousness begins to stir in our awareness. The statements that *"Many are called but Few are chosen"* is symptomatic of the acceptance of Free Will. We tend to equate Free Will with our ability of manipulate phenomenal reality. This simply means that we no longer blame others for our station in life. We begin to realize that we, and we alone, create the reality in which we live. However... by the way, we are not free to break the Universal Laws. Even 'gods' can't do that!

This is the beginning of the end.

The end of being a transient part of the *Result* and the beginning of being an inseparable part of the immortal *Cause*.

This is true, though only to a degree.

All aspects of the phenomenal reality are by nature transient. Next we learn that in spite of, or perhaps because of, the transiency of the world we live in, we become aware that there are no rewards or punishments in our reality. We also become aware, however, that there are completely unavoidable consequences.

We discover that there is no religious carrot or stick awaiting us on dying. Instead, there is the unforgiving Law of Karma. Having lost faith in an all-forgiving, infinitely benevolent, deity that repairs if not atones for all our transgressions, for the first time we are forced to take total responsibility for our actions.

Then for our emotions.

Then for our thoughts.

Yes, we learn that thoughts and emotions are at the root of all energies that metamorphose all energies of our reality.

We learn that *"As you sow, so shall you reap"* is a golden truth.

Karma is the eternal, irrepressible equalizer that restores balance, necessary for (even transient) preservation of our reality. What should be noted, however, is that the Law of Karma restores only the Universal balance, not the inadequacies of personal disingenuousness. We are expected to restore our own state of balance. To repay our own debts.

Our Universe may be transient, but it is NOT up to us to determine the duration of its vitality and exuberance. As mentioned previously, the centripetal and centrifugal forces define the range within which we must work—the extent to which we can contribute to diversity. It is safer to work within the Straight and Narrow, or the temporal, spatial, and philosophical limits of the Event Horizon.

Within these parameters, we are intended to have fun.

After all, we are supposed to enjoy "free will" (within the confines of the Universal Laws) that we once enjoyed in the "Garden of Eden", wherein our Consciousness was free beyond our present limitations. There and then, at that stage of our evolutions, we had been guided only by the laws of nature. By the Universal Laws. Then, we evolved a brain capable of generating an Ego. Also, we forgot that just a billion or two years ago we were no more than monocellular organisms. As you've already read in Chapter 3, our brain doubled its storage capacity when Eve was 'born'—when our hermaphrodite nature was split into two complementary halves.

Evolution advances in mysterious ways.

Yet I suspect that even in Paradise, within the Consciousness of almost unlimited freedom, there were (and are) consequences. The laws of Cause and Effect discovered by Isaac Newton were the basis of the phenomenal reality. For every action there is an equal and opposite reaction. The balance will be respected. Yet these laws apply only to the causative energies which contradict the Universal Laws.

What Free Will really refers to is the discovery and the acceptance of our heritage. We, and we alone, decide to be among the Chosen Few, by aligning our Ego with our Self. When we accept the immortality of our Self, we accept the transiency of our becoming, of our Ego. We become immortal by changing our point of view. Once we place our attention on our Self, our reality changes diametrically. We enter the "Kingdom of Heaven" while still here, on Earth.

The phenomenal reality becomes a transient illusion.

I wonder if this is what Albert Einstein meant.

Or perhaps this is just the consequence of choosing the truth.

Nevertheless, the Garden of Eden, was a state of Consciousness akin to Paradise. We have been created, then evolved, to be happy.

Here and now.

Yet, we got kicked out of Paradise. Knowledge gives power, and power corrupts unless is it held in the reins of steel. Or... *balanced by Unconditional Love.* This lesson had been given to us in the previous Zodiac Age of Pisces.

History teaches us that, since then, from time immemorial, people searched for happiness. The 'lost' happiness? There are countless writers, preachers, philosophers, psychologists, even poets, all assuring us that they can supply us with the elixir of the gods. People even resort to drugs, strange customs, food and drinks, all to sate their need for happiness.

Women are lucky.

Their love for their children is built into their genes. And, it seems to be the most perfect, the unconditional love. It fails very rarely, and it is not limited to human species only. It is the creative energy that encompasses virtually all living creatures and assures the survival of most species.

As for men, there are ample examples of mystics, who appeared to have enjoyed happiness, in fact joy, regardless of the conditions in which they conducted their becoming. When we become aware of the mystery of their state of mind, we will have reached the beginning of the end—the end of our childhood. We shall find inklings of the unlimited power within our Consciousness.

Allow me to assure you of one thing.

The moment we become completely aware and convinced of our immortality, things change. One unavoidable benefit is a state of happiness. Most of the time, it is like being in Heaven. *Here and Now.*

We become apprentice gods.

In the meantime, we must never forget that life is synonymous with continuous change. This applies to our cellular, atomic and sub-atomic structure, never forgetting that all is energy. As such, it is also vital that our mind continues to expand its capacity.

Maintaining *status quo* in any of these fields accelerates death. Let us remember that life is an expression of Consciousness. No matter how noble our concepts may be, the consequence of mental stagnation is mental death. It is known as Alzheimer.[(2)]

~~~

(1) My webpage is at http://stanlaw.ca. It will direct you too various retailers. I hope to see you often!

(2) My familiarity with Alzheimer is described in my novel, which you can examine on my webpage: *GATE—Things my Mother told Me.* https://stanlaw.ca

Chapter 20
INVETERATE DUALITY
(Why We Shall Be: Phase Three)

> *"I'd rather entrust the government of the United States to the first 400 people listed in the Boston telephone directory than to the faculty of Harvard University."*
> **William Frank *Buckley*, Jr. (1925 - 2008)**
> American author and commentator.

> *"The distinction between the past, present and future is only a stubbornly* persistent illusion."
> *"Reality is merely an illusion, although a very persistent one."*
> **Albert Einstein (1879 - 1955)**
> Nobel Prize in Physics in 1921

> *"The only real valuable thing is intuition."*
> **Albert Einstein (1879 - 1955)**
> Nobel Prize in Physics in 1921

> *"Learn from yesterday, live for today, hope for tomorrow. The important thing is not to stop questioning."*
> **Albert Einstein (1879 - 1955)**
> Nobel Prize in Physics in 1921

There are only ***Two Immutable Universal Laws*** that dominate the phenomenal reality. The first is ***Singularity*** and the second is ***Diversity***. In the phenomenal reality they are expressed as the centripetal and centrifugal forces. The first maintains our unity, the second assures diversity and the resulting expansion. *All* other laws are byproducts of these two primary Laws. We must construct our reality based on these two premises. If successful, they will lead us back to Eden.

And what is Eden?

It is a state of Consciousness which inspires us to act in a manner such as to sustain these two Universal Laws, and none other. All other animals are still responding to their dictates. All except the humans.

Can we control our destiny?
We are now facing two distinct possibilities.
The first is that we are a conglomeration of trillions of cells which take nutrients from food, convert them into energy and carry out specialized functions for no apparent reason other than to feed an average of 100 trillion microbes in and on our bodies which appear to wage a constant battle for and against the welfare of our bodies.

All this is for no other reason than to keep us 'alive'.

The second option is that our bodies have some other purpose. A purpose, for instance, to create and maintain an artificial intelligence, which would enable us, in time, to cooperate with the Creative Energy which created and assembled us (our bodies) in a most intricate fashion. A purpose other than to feed the hundred trillion cells of microorganisms, essentially of bacteria.

I side with the second option.

Yet if so, we enter a field of knowledge which, to a great extent, is still unknowable to us. After all, our neurons don't know much, other than how to be neurons. Only their intricate collection and the continuous firing of those electrochemical synapses seem to generate an artificial intelligence which strives to find out... [1]

...what happened?
Who or what am I?
How did I get here?
Why... and what for?

The questions never end. But the first conclusion we reach is that all this complexity could not have happened by accident. Sooner or later we shall conclude that some sort of intelligence must have been involved, which continues to guide the behaviour pattern of those trillions of cells to some, as yet unknown, purpose—even if this makes us just a little more than biological robots.

And this leads us to the problem of inexplicable **Duality of Creation.** We embody energies of **Being & Becoming.** They are expressed by three attributes of our mind, the:

The Conscious, Subconscious and the Unconscious
Energies.

Yes. They are all energies at very different rates of vibration, no matter how intangible they are. Together, they control our phenomenal reality.

These are in addition to the *artificial consciousness* generated by our brain. To make it quite clear, the mind, which is an attribute of the **Omnipresent Consciousness**, created the brain, not the other way round.

The energy of **Consciousness** abides in the *eternal present*. It is the attribute of what is sometimes referred to as our *Higher Self*. The **Subconscious** is the repository of the *eternal past*. And the third, the **Unconscious**, is our only connection to the *eternal potential (*hence *future)*.

Although it seems hard to reconcile, they are all extant only in the **Eternal Present**. In the... NOW. To cheer you up, the Theory of quantum mechanics appears to be just as incomprehensible.

"If you think you understand quantum mechanics, you don't understand quantum mechanics," he said.[3] And they gave him a Nobel Prize for it.

Well... almost for it!

As suggested, the Subconscious is the storehouse of memories and it generates *instinct*. The Unconscious is the birthplace of *intuition*.

CONCLUSIONS

While our Being (Self) abides in the eternal present, in the NOW, our artificial intelligence (Ego) is capable of recognizing only a fragment of eternity at a time, hence the necessity of the past and the future. Nevertheless, we can only experience our Being, our Higher Self, in the present.

In the process of Becoming we use the AI in everyday affairs, and to sustain our Becoming in the phenomenal Universe. All four energies are imperative to our life. All four, as Albert Einstein assured us, are forms of energy. The first three are real, the last, and only the last, is illusory. Yet, allow me to assure you, that to be able to partake in the process of Becoming is a most incredible gift. You might say, that in partaking in Life, we are the inseparable, integral 'children' of, what the Bible calls, the Living God.

No matter how much we might deny it, we consist of the inner and the outer expressions of our Being, which is the individualization of the energy of the Omnipresent Consciousness. The inner, the intangible energy of Consciousness that is beyond the limitations of the phenomenal reality, is in a static condition, yet it can be thought of as the kinetic energy.[2]

However, as even in the phenomenal reality the energy of Consciousness is Omnipresent, its kinetic properties are not sustained by movement in either space or time, but are due, solely, to the rate of vibration it maintains. As its rate of vibrations is infinite, it is at the source of all other energies, which have influence on its expression in phenomenal reality. The only energy that does appear to influence its metamorphosis to slower rates of vibration is the energy of thought, generated by the energy of the Mind. Hence, the Mind appears to be equally omnipresent. Or, at least, wherever it manifests itself, the elements of phenomenal reality begin to appear. The energy of thought forms are the building blocks of the World we live in.

And this is where we came in.
Thus the question raised in *DELUSIONS*:
"Why we shall be?"

Whether we think well or badly has no bearing. Thought affects the creative energy of Consciousness. In fact, as suggested, thoughts create the reality in which we conduct our Becoming. They create the reality in which we live.

This in no way affects our Being, which remains detached from all transient forms that we create with our thoughts. What thoughts do affect is the reality in which our Ego, generated by our brain, conducts the process of Becoming—the process of ever-changing, continuously metamorphosing, hence eternally illusory nature of our life.

Life is change.

Change is caused by the metamorphosis of energy.

The metamorphosis is the result of the change in the rate of vibrations. What we continuously seem to forget is the indubitable fact that, in the midst of this whirlwind of metamorphosis, our Consciousness of Being remains static.

The *I AM* never changes.

What changes, continuously, is the phenomenal reality. And this is caused by our thoughts. Hence:

We must be
very careful what we think.

Whatever it is, the reality we create is the reality we'll live in until we change it with our thoughts. No matter how illusory it might be in the 'scientific' sense, we'll recognize it as real. This is the limitation of the intelligence generated by our brain.

Thoughts are energy.

According to Einstein, energy cannot be destroyed. It can, however, metamorphose into endless forms, or expressions, of phenomenal reality. Every time we watch "entertainment" on TV, exploiting murder, crimes, theft, any forms of debauchery, or any other diminution of our ultimate potential, the thoughts we experience, hence generate, contribute to the nature of our reality.

Like attracts like, even if against our will.

Being thoughtless is just as destructive. It allows negative reality to continue. Also, it wastes our greatest gift.

It must be mentioned, indeed stressed, that the creative power which results in the *objective* reality, that appears real to us, is stabilized by more than one person accepting this reality at the same time. The Universe we behold in the night sky is the result of the visual images perceived and imagined for billions of years by countless billions of intelligent beings such as we are... (though I often have serious doubts about human intelligence). Regrettably, or perhaps by intent, the biblical expression comes to mind once again: *"Many are called, but only few are chosen."*

And then, of course, there is my addition of the *"Third Party"* who have not, as yet, even been called. They are the sheep who follow their (often pathetic) leaders and accept their images, unwittingly giving additional substance to the reality created by others.

If only they'd follow the Few...

Let us never forget that Eden, Heaven, and Hell are all states of Consciousness. They are not way out, there, yonder, beyond our reach, accessible only to the dead. They are diverse states of Consciousness of unlimited choices which we create while here, on Earth, being very much alive. We experience the foretaste of 'Heaven' each night, during REM (rapid eye movement) phases of sleep, when the brain activity is high, similar to that when we're awake. An average person can experience dreams from three to five times a night. They can last from a few seconds to 20 or 30 minutes, although during dreaming the dimension of time is greatly extended. Memories of hours of dream-time may have taken place during no more than a few minutes.

The state of consciousness that we experience during our dreams are characterized by changes in all four dimensions. This is due to a higher rate of vibration of the reality we experience.

Ultimately, we shall begin to believe that we are creating these realities. We shall begin to do so consciously. While wide awake. We shall experience the power of the gods.

It is all up to us.

And this is *why we shall be*. To meet our destiny. To enhance the phenomenal Universe we live in. To have fun!

It is vital to stress one other point.

The FEW do not exhibit any moral or ethical traits as defined by human standards. The FEW refers *only* to their ability to metamorphose the source Energy, the Energy of Omnipresent Consciousness, and other ensuing energies, to diversify but not necessarily enhance the Universe. This diversification remains, though hopefully progressively to a lesser degree, a process of trial and error.

'Sins', (missing the mark) are permitted, though not encouraged. Ultimately, balance must be restored and maintained.

Also, remember the *Event Horizon*?

By 'human' ethical or moral standards our contributions can be good, bad, or indifferent. However, there is no 'human' morality in the Universal equation. We diversify and enhance, or we don't. These two factors define our usefulness to the Whole.

It is worth mentioning that each time we wake up in the

morning, the awakening is comparable to another fragmentary cyclic reincarnation. The only difference is that very few of us can remember our previous lives. On the other hand, in my experience, very few of us can remember our dreams either.

It should be mentioned that we can effect quite amazing feats once we master the ability of lucid dreaming, the results of which can be carried over to our waking state. There are countless examples of people who have done it. Likewise, we can, and often do though usually unknowingly, benefit from accomplishments in our previous lives. Such benefits are particularly noticeable in the so-called, wonder children (wunderkind), who manifest abilities at a very early age. Child prodigies often go unnoticed, or are relegated to unknown, and still misunderstood states of consciousness, such as autism.

~~~

(1) Although, recently, more power had been assigned to a single neuron.

(2) In physics, the **kinetic energy** (KE) of an object is the **energy** that it possesses due to its motion. In metaphysics, KE is the energy it possesses due to its *rate of vibration*. Hence the energy of Consciousness, vibrating at infinite rate, is the most powerful force in the Universe.

(3) Richard Feynman

~~~~~~~

[THE UNIVERSITY is the last part of excerpts adapted from *Beyond Religion 1, Essay #52*. As with KINDERGARTEN and THE SCHOOL it offers pertinent answers rather than raising questions. I include it for people who may not have had a chance to read *DELUSIONS—Pragmatic Realism*. If you are already familiar with it, please move onto the next chapter.]

THE UNIVERSITY
(Excerpts from Beyond Religion 1, Essay #52)

The biological answer is simple: we shall continue to be because our genes are immortal. As my friend said the other day, "morons marry morons and produce more morons". But that is not really what I want to talk about. I wish to discuss reasons why we shall be what we shall be due to the evolution of our Consciousness—of the (artificial) consciousness generated by our brain.

It may have escaped notice of some of my readers that the word 'university' comes from Latin, *universitas*, meaning "the whole" (world), or the universe. Hence, there is part three of our evolution, at least the evolution of some of us, and hopefully, ultimately, all of us. Let us never forget that we alone decide if we wish to be the chosen ones. Natural selection is concerned with physical survival and thus with quantity.

The rest is up to us.

Those of us who do decide to continue will have an effect on, and be affected by, the whole universe. This may include any number of universes the scientists discover, as they go along. Perhaps as many universes as there are individualized states of Consciousness. Yet, when all is said and done, there is only One Omnipresent Consciousness, hence only one phenomenal Universe consisting of as many parts as there are atoms in human body. For those of you who like numbers, that's about seven billion billion billion atoms, or a 7 followed by 27 zeros. And when you finish counting the stars, or the atoms in your body, someone will think of adding a new diversity to the phenomenal world, and it will expand the Universe still farther.

And if you don't like my summary, the present,

observable though ever-expanding universe is said to include about 10 billion galaxies. Assuming an average of some 100 billion stars in each galaxy, we end up with one billion trillion stars. Or:

$$1,000,000,000,000,000,000,000$$

if you prefer numerical expression. Be my guest! But remember, that's only the observable universe. I'm sure we can triple this number when we improve our technology, although, I have no idea why we should.

I mentioned earlier that while in SCHOOL the teacher was, if often unsuccessfully, responsible for our learning process, while in the UNIVERSITY the onus lies squarely on our shoulders. We alone can decide if we wish to evolve, and to continue evolving, and Darwin has very little to do with our progress. We are no longer relying on nature equipping us with the necessary appurtenances to get down from trees, to hunt for our prey (dinner), or even to combat the bacteria, viruses and a host of other bugs, which might threaten to enhance or... terminate our wellbeing. To give credit where credit is due, most of us will arrive at the university with a superb immune system. Nevertheless, by now we are intended to rely on our brain—mind, if you prefer—to take care of our needs.

Regrettably, not every member of our species appears to know that, and they will pay the price for their ignorance. There is an old adage stating: *"Ignorance of the law is no excuse for breaking it."* This law applied throughout our evolution, voluntarily or imposed on us by nature, and/or by the Universal Laws. Regretfully, also by those who take it upon themselves to subjugate those they regard weaker than they are. Let us never forget that, more often than not, "bad governments are elected by good people who don't vote." I didn't invent this adage, but it sounds very convincing.

Thus, responsibility reverts to us.

Always!

We must also never forget the biblical statement that *"many are called but few are chosen."* Mother Nature is cruel. Not every acorn will grow into an oak tree. Not every seed will bear fruit. Not every member of the *Homo sapiens* (not always very *sapient*) species will reach his or her intended potential. That's how nature works: in incredible abundance, in the hope that at least some of her plans will be fulfilled.

We know that our bodies are recycled 'material' (energy). Who knows what happens to our individualized states of Consciousness? We know that they are immortal, but can they return to their Source, even as every drop of rain will ultimately return to the Ocean?

Furthermore nature is most absurdly wasteful, or generous, if you hold God or Darwin responsible for creation.

Sometime ago, an article from the *Washington Post* was reprinted in my local newspaper. It announced the results of an extensive scientific research, which stated that: *"Most newly conceived human embryos harbor colossal genetic defects that are incompatible with life."* Furthermore, *"...most pregnancies—whether naturally occurring or the result of test-tube fertilization — quietly fail within days or a few weeks after conception."*

That's only a small part of it. Yet in *God Delusion* Richard Dawkins writes:

> *"Religion is so wasteful, so extravagant; and Darwinian selection habitually targets and eliminates waste. Nature is a miserly accountant, grudging the pennies, watching the clock,*

punishing the smallest extravagance."

Please read on. It seems that Messrs. Darwin and Dawkins live on different planets.

An average (human) male produces between two and six milliliters of semen in each ejaculation. This adds up to between 200 and 500 million sperm cells. Let us accept a conservative average of 300 million cells. Multiply that by say, 2 billion males, then by, say, 52 ejaculations per year.

Do your own math.

300,000,000 x 2,000,000,000 x 52 = the number of sperm cells wasted by males of our species alone in a single year. Less the successful impregnations, of course—one per year per male, say. For a few years.

Then? Zilch!

Contrary to the expert testimony of Richard Dawkins, nothing is a wasteful as nature.

On the other hand, perhaps we should add some 2 billion men, boys really, who are going through their teen masturbatory years. That should add a good few trillion wasted sperm cells. After all, nature disposes teenagers by *very natural selection* to do so, right? Naturally, the boys might prefer to select girls; but usually, not for the lack of trying, they are not given a chance.

Perhaps, "Me too" took care of that. [1]

Surely, my figures are *very* conservative, yet wastage is staggering by any standard. By contrast, women produce but a few eggs at a time; yet even then, most go by the wayside. They are also wasted. The profusion of nature's squander is flabbergasting. Perhaps in another few million years it will improve its batting average. At present, nature's idea of Pragmatic Realism is to produce everything in such abundance that at least some of them are going to work. Survive? A most primitive trial and error technique.

"...punishing the smallest extravagance" ???

Speak for yourself, Dr. Dawkins. I strongly suspect that some of Dawkins's neurons have been eliminated by nature.

I'd suggest that evolution advances by habitually destroying it's own creation. Don't get me wrong. I do not disagree with natural selection. I do disagree with juxtaposing it to religion in any way whatsoever. Perhaps nature ought to listen to the architect Mies van der Rohe, who advocated the maxim that "less is more". He was also talking about creation; only he referred to buildings.

And then, Dawkins adds on the same page:

"Nature cannot afford frivolous jeux d'esprit."

My goodness! At the risk of being frivolous, I read somewhere that, with regards to masturbation, there are only two types of men in the world. Those who admit to doing it, and those who don't admit it. That leaves, say, 3 billion men who do (the rest of the population are women and children). Let us multiply this number by some 300 million sperm at each ejaculation, and then say, again, by (a minimum?) of 52 weeks per year, and we have an elegant image of nature's idea of *jeux d'esprit*.

This seems to fall somewhat short of the "traditional interpretations of Darwinism, in which 'benefit' is assumed to mean benefit for individual survival and reproduction."

Unless, of course, Darwin and Dawkins exclude the human species from the evolutionary equation. Wouldn't that be interesting? Although in the case of some people, who'll remain nameless, this might be close to the truth.

Just to recap. To make Pragmatic Realism work in the evolutionary sense, nature has devised a system referred to by Charles Darwin and his followers as natural selection. The system relies on its self-perpetuation, on the production of sperm/seed/acorn in such a profusion, with such abandon, that at least one sperm/seed/acorn might be malformed, which in turn might result in a mutation, which, if it survives, which is doubtful, might result in… an evolutionary advancement.

Or not.

Or it might prove inferior to the *status quo*.

Of course, some seed/acorns might be eaten by other wasteful organisms. As for human sperm, no one in their wildest dreams could accuse nature of exhibiting even a smidgen of intelligence in its method.

Unless…

…unless, regardless of what nature does with the rest of her creative profusion, from the evolutionary point of view, humans', sole purpose, is to serve as milking cows for microorganisms, mostly bacteria, who, or which, indulge their gustatory tastes in the epicurean delight of our sperm.

The rest of the time, we can walk about picking up poop after our dogs. (If you want to find our true purpose in the canine reality, I refer you to *"Broohos"* in my *Cats and Dogs* stories.)

We, you and I, are part of nature. At least physically. For some of us, that's all we are. Wasters? Or are we, some of us, more than that?

Dawkins and all his cohorts deal exclusively with the phenomenal reality which, according to Albert Einstein, is an illusion.

At the University stage, we become students. We discover that our newly found freedom is commensurate with our acceptance of responsibility. We no longer hold teachers, preachers, priests, confessors, psychologists, politicians, our parents, or even circumstances responsible for our survival. In fact, our definition of survival is undergoing a fundamental change. The temporal extension of our physical life is no longer our priority.

Quality takes preference over quantity.

We begin to suspect, then know, that we are entities with an unimaginable potential. We learn from every quarter, from the past and the present, from nature, from the positive and negative traits still integral to our mental, emotional and physical embodiments.

We learn the difference between reactive and causative action.

We refuse to conform for the sake of the illusion of security we used to derive from the concept of belonging to a group.

We become individuals.

Even as the preceding phases of our evolution dealt with survival within constraints of time and space, they were also confined to specific duration. Our university, however, deals with that which has neither beginning nor end. It finds its reality outside constraints of the space/time continuum. This realization empowers us to step outside our material limitations.

Outside our physical bodies.

From this new vantage point, we observe the forces controlling our environment. We observe the rich becoming richer, the poor—poorer. Only we no longer measure wealth by the old yardstick of money or fame or power. Those who are happy—increase in their joy; the miserable—tend to sink into depression. *Regardless of circumstances.* We became aware of the universal rule that, unwittingly, controlled us from the moment we became enwrapped in material reality:

WE ARE THE PRODUCT OF OUR CONTEMPLATION.

We note that every thought we entertain influences our

reality. Every thought we energize with emotion defines our future. We learn to control our thoughts. We become selective in the use of, and learn to control, our emotions. We learn that to realize a dream, we must have a dream. To reach a goal, we must have a goal. To realize the impossible, we must believe that, within the Universal Laws, *everything* is possible. We become the conscious effect of the creative power of our beliefs. We perceive that at every instant of existence, we are the consequence of our past, the forerunners of our futures.

We take control.

Growing we grow, maturing we mature, ever reaching for the eternally receding horizon. Slowly, so very slowly, it dawns on us that there are no horizons. We realize that we, ourselves, define the characteristics and the scope of our reality. We realize that we create the Universe in which we design our Becoming.

The lightning strikes.

Time stops.

We begin living in the present.

There may be another mode to our existence. As the universe seems to be almost empty of matter, we may find, in time, the secret of the great mystics of the past. (See the 'Postscript' to *DELUSIONS*)

What if the whole Universe, including our human bodies, were to be the result of the creative energy (spirit, if you like) unfolding itself in a pragmatic way? What if it were an ongoing process that seems to have had neither a beginning nor a predictable end? All manner of creation is endowed with the ability to act in accordance with the Universal Laws, inherent in the creative energy itself. It is discernible in everything, including human animals. We have begun in a reactive mode of Becoming.

And then *"unto us a child is born."*

This is a wondrous phrase, already discussed above (Chapter 18), in which the prophet Isaiah describes his own experience. I beg your indulgence to look at it once more:

"For unto us a child is born, unto us a son is given: and the government shall be upon his shoulder: and his name shall be called Wonderful, Counsellor, The mighty God, The everlasting Father, The Prince of Peace."

Let us examine this phrase in detail. First of all, it all deals with states of Consciousness, *i.e.,* the only permanent reality. The 'child' symbolizes the first awareness that we may, just may, be more than just flesh and bones. This thought alone grows into such confidence that, instead of listening to priests and other men of authority, we begin to trust our own Self. We no longer defer to outside sources to know how to act.

As our confidence rises still further, we begin to realize that this power that has awakened within us is quite inexplicably wonderful. We began to trust in our judgment not just in decisions concerning our everyday affairs, but also in matters of greater and greater importance; in matters affecting the welfare of others; of our whole environment. Even as we learn to do so, even as our confidence grows, we feel the stirring of unlimited power welling within us.

We feel that nothing is impossible for us.

And then, surprisingly, we realize that this power was always dormant within us, and that it is that power and not what we thought we were that brought about this change within us. We begin to suspect that this authority, this ability, was always there, only it took us a long time to realize it, to become aware of it, and then to accept it. It and we became inseparable, indistinguishable. We became One. At this stage we realize that, in fact, we always were One. And this immutable knowledge gives us a most extraordinary,

unearthly feeling of peace.
Peace beyond human understanding.

The perceiver and the perceived become one.

Actually, they always were. Whether one reaches this realization in one's present life, or a million years from now, it matters little. That which waits dormant within us is immortal. It has its being outside the confines of time and space. It changes its external sheath until a suitable one is ready. Then, and only then, this euphoric union takes place.
So said Isaiah some 2,700 years ago.
One can but wonder how many people listened.

This process, described so poetically by the Prophet Isaiah, should never be confused with the condition described by the American psychologist Julian Jaynes, which he also appears to associate with the growth of human consciousness. In his observations, there are external voices that insinuate themselves into our heads and imbue us with a reality supported by such voices, sometimes accompanied by hallucinatory images. The condition he describes is reminiscent of schizophrenia or some other deeply seated psychosis.
The above statement by the Prophet Isaiah has nothing to do with such images, sounds, or explanations. Any externalization, or dichotomy, taking place at any stage of the growing realization of our true nature would immediately throw us into the waiting arms of the religious proselytizers. We would immediately fall into the clutches of religion. The only method of reaching the state of Consciousness offered by Isaiah is a lonely, lonesome, individual journey. No two people can reach the same level of realization of the infinite. That is why, perhaps, there are so many of us, scattered throughout the multiverse.
But we should have no delusions.

Those who are not yet aware of the wondrous child, of the potential dormant within us—Yeshûa called dead. ("*Let the dead bury the dead,*" remember?) But there is hope. They are not *already* dead, but *still* dead. Not yet awakened. Like Buddhas in waiting.

Let us consider that the man who is describing his new awareness is said to have lived between 759 and 690 BC, yet his evolutionary level vastly exceeded most men I've met to this day. He obviously states that, with a little effort, we can reach out towards our infinite potential. The only god he recognized was within his Consciousness. Yeshûa, of course, reiterated the same sentiment later. People, religionists, churches, and… scientists, continued to look for that infinite potential outside their own being. Hence, disappointment and abject deism or atheism—two sides of the same coin.

According to Isaiah, this new state of consciousness is making us aware that we are each, individually, one with and inseparable from the total, universal, omnipresent Consciousness, which brings about the transient condition of eternal Becoming. This new Consciousness, this new awareness, this new 'child' is one with and indivisible from the Omnipresent Consciousness.

A fraction of the infinite is still infinite. All the attributes are the same. They are indivisible.

All the knowledge is already within us. It is only a question of recall.

~~~

(1) The *Me Too* (or *#MeToo*) was a movement against sexual harassment and sexual assault, initially used in this context on social media in 2006.

Chapter 21
GOOD, EVIL, & IMMORTALITY
(Scientist's Delusion)

> *"Tell him to live by yes and no — yes to everything good, no to everything bad."*
> **William James (1842 - 1910)**
> (As quoted in *The Thought and Character of William James* by Ralph Barton Perry)

> *"Let your Yea be Yea; and your Nay, Nay."*
> **Matthew 5:33 (KJV)**

> *"I dreamed I was a butterfly. Then I awoke. Now I wonder. Am I a man who dreamt of being a butterfly, or a butterfly dreaming that I am a man?"*
> **Chuang Tzu (399 - 295 BC)**
> Chinese philosopher

As mentioned in previous chapter, let us repeat this maxim to make it abundantly clear. There is no such thing as "Good or Evil". At best, evil might be considered to be the absence of good, but even then the concept of good must be considerably redefined.

Good is only that which is good for the phenomenal Universe,

not what might be good for any individual at the expense of another. Good is that which expands through creativity, and enhances the nature of our Universe, through balance, order, and beauty. All else will eventually be recycled.

Also, our scientists are baffled by the ever-expanding

Universe. Not only does it expand (they say), but it does so at an ever-increasing pace. The expansion, as discussed in Chapter 7, continues to accelerate.

The problem with scientists is that their only ambition is knowledge. Regrettably, they seek only the knowledge of the phenomenal Universe. That alone was, and continues to be, the Apple of Eden. That and the resulting pride. Whereas the only purpose for which we were brought to life is to discover Heaven within us. Heaven within our Consciousness. This is also how we enhance the Universe—by creating a Heaven within our Consciousness, which is the only true reality. Heaven within which our "Father", the Immortal, Infinite Creative Energy, flourishes, ever ready, willing, and able to add to the diversity of the phenomenal Universe. Ever ready, willing, and able to enhance the phenomenal Universe for our other Selves residing in an infinity of other beings, other entities individualized within the phenomenal Universe, until we make it as perfect as the Infinite Potential demands of us.

And... to avoid the mistake that 'Adam' had made.

Let us remember that Eve symbolizes our subconscious, and our subconscious is the sum-total of our memories, hence experience and the resulting knowledge from the beginning of our countless incarnations, from the day that we became aware that the Omnipresent Consciousness is also present within us.

That we are Its Individualizations.

That's an enormous burden of the past. Yet, as we know, life abides only in the present. In the Eternal NOW.

We can begin by watching the fauna and flora which still reside in Paradise. Our true and only home.

So what of Good or Evil?

As I keep repeating, the Universe demands of us that we contribute to its diversity, and enhance it in the process of doing so. That's it. There are no other ethical postulates that should or might control our life. All else are 'human' invention (products of AI). They are elaborated mostly by various religious groups for the purpose of controlling the behaviour of the "Third Party", *i.e.,* of the vast majority of people.

The reason why human attributes of good and evil do not apply to Universal Laws is that the Universal Laws apply *only* to the PROCESS, not to the consequences or the results of this process. In the phenomenal reality, life is only thing that counts.

Life is the process of continuous change.

Once an item, a thing, or even a living entity has been created, the Universal Laws no longer apply and HUMAN laws take over. Human Laws are designed to sustain and maintain the *status quo*, while the Universal Laws encourage change which produces diversity. To repeat, in the phenomenal reality only life, *ergo* CHANGE, matters. The *status quo* is maintained by the Universal Consciousness through the Law of balance. Of equilibrium.

Hence the Event Horizon.

Nevertheless, Human Laws, inadequate though they be, are necessary to give the phenomenal reality an illusion of stability.

At this stage of our evolution we need this ephemeral stability to retain our sanity. To live in a world of Einstein's illusion would drive the vast majority of us crazy. Only the Few are ready.

And now, finally, I'll share with you a secret you probably will not believe for many years to come. Perhaps, for many reincarnations.

There is no death.

When I began writing this silent soliloquy, I was jealous of the great people who 'died' young. Not just Jesus Christ, but artists, composers, actors, even sportsmen... All famous for having done a great deal in a very short time. Perhaps they had fulfilled their destiny, their dharma, and had been transferred, or had earned the right to continue their Becoming in a higher reality.

Perhaps...

But then I realized that although this might apply to some of them, there could be another explanation.

Having achieved a great deal, some of them might have stopped evolving—and life demands that we do evolve. They transferred to us all their potential to us that they had been intended to transfer.

Alternatively, those of us who continue to learn might be not punished but rewarded with long life—for as long as we learn, no matter how slowly. While learning we increase our potential of adding diversity to the Universe. After all, in essence, time does not really exist, remember?

It also seems to me that only those who listen to that man who died at the age of 34 might be rewarded with long life.

The man who had said:

"Heaven is within you."

Today I know that I do not have to die to advance to Heaven or any other reality of a higher rate of vibrations. Although I'm sure it would be nice and satisfying to extend the freedom I experience in my dreams in full Consciousness, finding the enchantment of Heaven within my Consciousness is, at least for now, enough for me.

On the other hand, there might be those who only serve as an example to others by producing things, or modes of behaviour, to avoid. Like trying to control others. We must always remember that the Universe subsists on a state of balance. This applies to all forms of energy, including that of dominance over "one's neighbour".

Are Empires compatible with the Universal Laws?

At its height, the British Empire was by far the largest empire in history. They wielded global power for almost a century. Only the Roman and Egyptian Empires lasted longer, although some claim that the Roman Empire is still influencing our lives.

Alas, many have never even heard about it!

Ignorance? Or... *sic transit Gloria mundi?*

And what are the consequences?

At present, in the UK, 850,000 people are said to be living with dementia. They estimate that, with an aging population this might rise to 1.5 million by 2040. Could it be just the consequence of running an Empire, or merely from upholding traditions, rather than going forward? After all, the Universal Laws demand change, progress, and enchantment. Did the British Empire enchant the Universe— or just the aristocracy of the day?

After all, we know how power corrupts...

On the other hand, in the US, the number of people who have succumbed to dementia already surpassed 5 million. Perhaps any kind of domination leads to the eventual loss of sanity. Or is the subliminal guilt so heavy that the ego tries to forget? All is energy, remember? So are memories. They even generate more memories. And, let's face it, the US does try to dominate the whole world. Is it already beginning to pay the price?

On the other hand, there may be other reasons for the increase in dementia. A popular program on TV (a medium I try to avoid), called *The Doctors*, pointed out that an early retirement may lead to dementia. While, due to my predisposition to switch off TV as soon as possible, I'm not sure what explanation the doctors offered, I drew my own conclusions. After all, one can be just as busy doing nothing much at home as one can in the office, in a factory, or supposedly digging for coal. It is a question of character, not the nature of the work.

No. It is not the retirement that causes dementia.

It is the absence of *new* challenges, *new* problems to solve. There is no observable increase of dementia among the members of the *Third Party*. Most of them seldom face challenging problems in their place of work. For them, most of what they do is carried out by a repetition of their acquired skills. They are the sustainers of the *status quo*. They can't lose what they haven't got.

The 'many', however, those who are already vaguely aware of their dharma, of their purpose, are challenged more often. Work provides an environment where such challenges are most likely to occur. It is the absence of *new* challenges which work provides for them that leads to the loss of mental faculties.

I played safe. On 'retirement' from architecture I decided to try something *new*. The 40 books I have published are the evidence that my faculties are still in working order.

(Although quite a few of my friends would challenge this claim!)

The wondrous thing about writing is that every book must be different, hence presenting new problems to solve. Otherwise there would be no reason for writing it. So what that in fiction they are mostly about illusions. Remember Einstein's view of this?

To sum up, only *new* challenges, *new* problems to solve, assure the continuous functioning of our mental faculties. Whatever they may be. Otherwise, with age, not only do our bodies lose their dexterity but so does our ability to use our brains. The old adage makes it clear:

"If you don't use it, you lose it."

We pay for all our mistakes. The phenomenal is a wonderfully balanced reality that refuses to be upset. We might even be paying for upholding many of our traditions. Nothing negates progress as efficiently as traditions. They repeat political, national, religious, cultural and many other modes of behaviour, ways of doing things, often proven mistakes (like famous battles, commemorations of human crimes, and suchlike) that protect at least the memories of the past, thus withholding progress.

Yes. Even victorious battles are mistakes. They do not enhance the Universe.

Sociologists affirm the positive aspects of some of our traditions. *"We must remember so that we don't repeat the same mistakes again,"* is their dictum. They forget that memories are energies that influence the present. Many more people remember the "Holocaust of the WWII" than the "Sermon on the Mountain." Why? Because remembering the Holocaust is a tradition, remembering the Sermon did not. Hence, the holocaust became ingrained in our psyche, the Sermon was not. Some traditions may even be positive. I may be wrong, but, perhaps, just perhaps... if the Sermon was a tradition, there might not have been any Holocaust...

And just look at our entertainment industry. Crime, murder, sexual abuse, brutality, corruption, theft... must I go on? They are the traditional inspirations/subject matters for our entertainment. It seems that art no longer imitates life.

> *"Life* imitating *art*. Anti-mimesis is a philosophical position that holds the direct opposite of Aristotelian mimesis. Its most notable proponent is Oscar Wilde, who opined in his 1889 essay *The Decay of Lying* that, "*Life* imitates *Art* far more than *Art* imitates *Life*". They *did* not exist till *Art* had invented them."

(Life imitating art - Wikipedia)

Yes, we, mostly the younger generation, imitate our TV heroes. Such perversions as are spewed at us by the entertainment industry must lead to our eventual demise. However, they already became a tradition.

A sick, decadent tradition.

To recap...

Life, as we know it, is the phenomenal expression of the indestructible energy that fosters change, hence DIVERSITY, which is one of the two fundamental Laws of the Universe. Since change through metamorphosis is the basic characteristic of the phenomenal Universe, it cannot be destroyed. There is only:

ONE UNIVERSAL CONSCIOUSNESS

And we are Its multitudinous expressions.

While the Creative Energy is Omnipresent, and defines the nature of all creation, we are given an extra commission.

Even as the human body maintains trillions of microorganisms within its tiny universe, so the Universal Consciousness manifests its desire for diversity through trillions of advanced phenomenal entities, vastly more advanced than we are, to manifest Its Potential.

Every intelligence, no matter how limited, serves to manifest the Potential to the degree it is capable. It is given such creative energies as it is capable of absorbing. In fact we can only manifest the gifts of which we become aware. Until we do, we are automatons reacting unwittingly to the Universal Laws.

And then, when all is said and done, there is the OBE. No. Not the *Order of the British Empire*. Let's face it, Empire is... no more. Empires come and go. The OBEs remain with us. I'm referring to something much harder to earn...

I'm referring to the *Out of Body Experience*. It is variously known as *OBE*, as *Soul Travel*, or as *Astral Projection*. There is, in my opinion, no greater proof of immortality than any of the above, which, essentially, are the same thing.

International Academy of Consciousness reported that they have evidence of out-of-body experience as a "real" or veridical phenomenon. In research related to the OBE, the *Princeton Engineering Anomalies Research* (PEAR) and the *Laboratory of Precognitive Remote Perception* (PRP) studies in 1987 already contained 334 formal trials with promising results. In his book, *End of Materialism*, Dr. Charles Tart, PhD, explains *"How Evidence of the Paranormal is Bringing Science and Spirit Together."*

Note the word *Evidence*.

On August 24th, 2016, scientists in Russia and Sweden reported breakthroughs confirming that Out-of-Body Experiences are real.[1]

All who haven't experienced OBE, will deny it. That is also true of people who don't believe that all is energy. That Consciousness is Energy. That energy can be metamorphosed into infinite rates of vibrations, thereby changing its nature and its characteristics. That they can run 100 meters in under 10 seconds. They are the non-believers.

And yet... many people have done it.

Have experienced it. And for those who have had experience of OBE, it has become an inerasable memory in their lives. Other than dreams, particularly lucid dreams, OBEs are by far the most explicit examples that all is energy.

Einstein's theories are finally confirmed by those Few.

It is always the *Few*. The Many and the Third Party vegetate behind until awakened. Perhaps biding their time? Yet, they also are needed. They also add to the diversity. And the Universe, as we know, thrives on diversity. There are now (in 2020) some 7.8 billion of us around. We shall reach 8 billion by 2026.

And who knows how many other intelligent beings proliferate (and enhance) the enormity of the phenomenal Universe?

As for the creation "in waiting", according to a new estimate there are about one trillion species of microbes on Earth, and 99,999% of them are still to be discovered! Evidently, the creative process is eternal.

We are still in the kindergarten, remember?

Yet, assuming evolution will not come to an untimely end, each of those microbes will one day evolve to be... human?

Surely, by then most of us will be gods!

And some, like us, have already embarked on the evolutionary trek:

*"To date, a total of 1.3 million species have been identified and described, but the truth is that many more live on Earth. The most accurate census, conducted by the Hawaii's University, estimates that a total of **8.7 million species** live on the planet."* [2]

As stated repeatedly, we are still in the kindergarten. In a Universe which, according to our juvenile cosmologists, is some 13.8 billion years old, we came down from trees only recently:

The earliest hominin, of presumably primitive bipedalism, is considered to be either Sahelanthropus or Orrorin, both of which arose some 6 to 7 million years ago. [3]

Hominids include orangutans, gorillas, chimpanzees, and human beings.

Now do you believe me? At least our embryonic birth took place earlier than the biblical reports. And now let us consider that the latest and brightest scientists have, at long last, reached the ancient Buddhists' conclusions that the Universe is eternal. If so, then we're just the latest experiment. Let's hope we succeed, although the rate at which devolution regresses is staggering.

[Please, don't tell anyone, but I enjoy being in the kindergarten. The Universe appears to be most forgiving. We seem to get away with almost anything. Like children.]

On the other hand, if we're regressing (becoming more materialistic or relying on illusion) then I can but wonder if other species have *Out of Body Experiences.* I know they dream. My cats do so on my lap, frequently, and their presumably involuntary movements indicate that their bodies perform spurts of great activity within their "dream bodies" while sleeping.

My wife gives me very similar indications.

Believe me. If you haven't already, learn OBE. You'll find all the instructions you need on the Internet. The rewards are staggering!

And now, finally, a joyful thought.

There is only one Omnipresent Consciousness. It may be individualized throughout the phenomenal Universe, but it remains One. We, all of us, continue to live within each other. My father and mother continue to live within me. (Their Consciousness is indestructible.) Your ancestors continue to experience life through you. And so forth. What if you have many children? Well, it may sound strange, but you continue to live within all of them. No, not within their bodies. Within their Consciousness. They are enriched by your presence.

Individualized Consciousness abides within and outside our phenomenal bodies.

In many ways, or in the most essential way, we are all One. God, or Father, or whatever name you assign to the Creative Energy, is in Heaven, and Heaven is within you. And within everyone of us, whether we discover It or not. This is the true reality.

And, as we all know, there is just one God.

One God within every single one of us. God is not a he or a she or an it. God is the Infinite Creative Potential that appears to individualize Itself, even if for a short while, in countless aspects of the phenomenal Universe. In fact, the Universe is the manifestation of that Infinite Energy which here, on Earth, and in all of the phenomenal Universe, is in a constant state of metamorphosis.

I am not a preacher, nor do I have the slightest intention of being nor becoming one. But if you make this philosophy the guideline for the rest of your life, you'll find happiness beyond human understanding.

Trust me.

I did.

~~~

(1) https://www.express.co.uk › News › Science

(2) https://allyouneedisbiology.wordpress.com › 2018/05/20 › biodiversity-species

(3) Human evolution — Wikipedia
https://www.express.co.uk › News › Science

POSTSCRIPTUM

> *"Men are so simple and so much inclined to obey immediate needs that a deceiver will never lack victims for his deceptions."*
> **Niccolo Machiavelli (1469 - 15270)**
> Florentine political philosopher, historian, musician, and poet

> *"The will to win, the desire to succeed, the urge to reach your full potential... these are the keys that will unlock the door to personal excellence."*
> **Confucius (551 - 479 BC)**
> Chinese philosopher and politician

> *"With realization of one's own potential and self-confidence in one's ability, one can build a better world."*
> **Dalai Lama**
> Spiritual leader of the Tibetan people

In *DELUSIONS-Pragmatic Realism*, I tended to point out our delusions derived, mostly, from our tendency to fall into the trap of fundamentalism. This tendency applied to both the religious and scientific societies. It is a direct consequence of the Edenic Apple, or, to bring it up to date, of intellectual pride.

There had been a time, long, long ago, when the priesthood were the keepers of all knowledge. The physics and metaphysics were treated as two aspects of reality—the aspect which we understood, and the aspect that we were still unable to understand. But make no mistake. Nobody, in our murky past, accepted things they did not understand as miracles. Such assumptions were born much later, when our egos couldn't accept that we are still abysmally ignorant.

Tell that to a PhD professor of physics and see what reaction you get. Why physics? Because most physicists still think that our reality consists of solid objects.

The concept that *"All is Energy"* came much later. In fact, most of us find it almost impossible to accept that the world we experience with our senses is an illusion. And... by the way, so are our senses.

We really are in a kindergarten of knowledge.

As always, there are exceptions. Albert Einstein and Richard Feynman come to mind. There are others, though only a few, so very few, who admit that we are still in the kindergarten of knowledge.

Somewhere in *DELUSIONS*, I may have suggested that there is only one thing that separates us from all the other life forms, and that it is our ability to choose. That the rest of life-forms are reactive. This is true, but only to a degree. While other species are subject to Universal Laws, so are we. The difference may lie only in the fact that we can oppose them knowingly, and pay the piper, whereas they pay the piper unknowingly.

They all think. All life-forms are equipped with the miracle of a functioning brain. Admittedly not as evolved as ours, although in some respects they exceed our resulting capability. Not one of us is capable of flying for thousands of miles to find the exact spot we visited last winter. Ducks can. As a matter of fact, we can't even fly. At least not unless we are hermetically sealed in a box, inhaling deeply, for hours on end, the accumulation of gas exuding from other people's alimentary canals.

Nor can we breathe under water. Well, nor can 75 species of dolphins, whales and porpoises yet they can live in the ocean. And while our sexual prowess has resulted in 7.8 billion primitive members of our species, none of us can live in the oceans. Yet 3.5 trillion fish can. This may not be of much interest to us unless the scientists confirm that global warming is true. It seems that they are already convinced. We not only can't breathe under water, but we can't breathe smoke either.

Since the industrial revolution we stopped evolving completely and became a species of gadgeteers. Rather than learning to do things, we design things to do things for us. We specialize in reducing our necessity of thinking to the minimum.

On the other hand, we appear to know (or kid ourselves?) *that* we think. Well most of us... Other species do not seem aware of their mental capacities. What other species are missing is their exorbitant ego. We think we own this world, this Earth. Our forefathers knew that we are only its guardians. Custodians. Curators. Administrators. Stewards or caretakers, but *never* its owners. And this is stated quite clearly in the Torah, that was NEVER intended to be usurped by sacerdotal fraternities for their personal ends.

Will the scourge of our egos forever stop us from doing our job? We are the "children of the Omnipresent Consciousness", just like everybody and everything else. Since the brightest from among our cosmologists and physicists finally realized that the phenomenal world is eternal, perhaps one day we shall realize that not so long ago we were little more than bacteria gallivanting at the hot outlets of underwater vents. We might also realize how many trillions of years lie ahead of us, before we shall become the creators of other worlds, other species, other diverse expressions of the Creative Energy.

For now, I think it's high time that our scientists stop experimenting on rodent brains on the assumption that their findings may also apply to us.

Our own puerile inadequacy can possibly be defined by a

single trait. Most of us still harbour an inherent inability to accept—hence believe, hence act as if we knew—that we are immortal. The convincing argument is quite simple. All is energy; energy is indestructible; we are energy. To repeat, if you don't believe me, ask Einstein.

That's it. What more do we need?

Our attitude changes diametrically, once we accept this premise. Better said, this *fact*. Our outlook at the whole of reality, at our past and possible future takes on a completely new understanding. There is no more eternal hell or heaven. There is only the Eternal Potential, and the Eternal Becoming.

The vital difference is the *process*.

As I keep repeating, all creation, no matter how wonderful, is transient. What matters is the creative act. We personify the Creative Energy. All else is an illusion. All else is transient.

For now, other species don't have this problem. Not yet. Ultimately they will. While today they represent the result, in the fullness of time they, too, will become conscious partakers in the creative process. Not all will make it. Some will refuse to grow, to evolve. Their energies will be recycled to a higher rate of vibration, to try again in the ever-expanding Universe.

Although unaware of it, other species still reside in Paradise. The Garden of Eden is not some sort of elusive Heaven invented by the sacerdotal societies. It is a reality which manifests at a much high rate of vibration. And, believe it or not, there are an infinite number of Heavenly realities. Most are such as we couldn't possibly even imagine. Infinity has neither beginning nor end.

Worlds without end.

...or beginning.

We know, or can know, that other species are still in

Paradise. We, due to our ego, have been kicked out. Although, according to Yeshûa, not for long. Or at least, not necessarily. After all, he assures us, Paradise remains within our Consciousness. We can return at any time.

And this is where I think I can offer a helping hand.

The only way we can be sure to find out way back to Paradise is to accept, unquestioningly, that we are immortal. To make it possible, we must accept that we are *not* our bodies, not just biological robots equipped with magnificent brains capable of generating artificial intelligence but, as Albert Einstein assured us, that we are energy. Pure, immortal, indestructible Energy.

Those who do not accept it will continue to live in fear of Ray Kurzweil's prognostications. The shadow of robots smarter than we are will hang, threateningly, over their future. And indeed, for some it may be true.

Yet, even then, those of us who accept that our purpose is only to enhance the phenomenal universe, we are just scratching the surface in the knowledge of our brain's potential. And we must never forget that acceptance of our immortality in no way absolves us from our principal, if not only, function. And our brain, which we are only just beginning to understand, is the tool we must use to fulfill our commission. A magnificent tool that shapes the infinite rate of vibration of Consciousness into the infinite possibilities in the phenomenal realities.

That's what being gods is all about.

A number of my readers had given me to understand that immortality is a spiritual concept. That if you accept it as your own nature, you become a religious person, probably with a halo around your head, who spends most of his or her time on his or her knees, in humble supplication for the forgiveness of his or her sins.

Well, the very opposite is true.

Once you know that you're immortal, this very trait becomes an intrinsic part of your nature. You are no longer a 'sinner'. Being immortal, you no longer expect rewards or punishments for your actions, but you know that you bear all the consequences of your actions.

You begin to grow up.

Just beginning. The road we travel never reaches the ever-retreating horizon. The joy is in the travel itself. In life. In our creative endeavours. That's what Paradise offers us. Think of all your dreams becoming a reality.

You know, without a shadow of a doubt, that Heaven and Hell are both states of Consciousness, and, what is more important, that none of them is eternal. For as long as the phenomenal Universe exists, your concept of Heaven, let alone Hell, will change. It will mature. Your awareness of Being and Becoming will gravitate closer together. And all this will be possible only because of the incredible biological computer housed in a small portion of your head.

Evelyn Monahan was right.

We are magnificent human beings, probably without equal in all creation.

Or at least, unequalled in this earthly Paradise created for our Becoming. Now that we know that we're immortal, it is our job to make it so.

And this takes us back to our brain which, for now, still remains an organ of many mysteries. Our continuous research into our neurons continually sheds new light on human intelligence and on our capabilities that we are far from using consciously.

We have already established that 86 billion of them communicate with each other. We also know that the dendrites are capable of solving complex problems on their own without engaging the rest of the neuron. And then we learned about the photons emitted apparently with ease.

So now we have to deal with the electrical impulses.

As photons are electromagnetic waves, they transmit electric and magnetic interactions. In communication, photons have a distinct advantage over electrons, which convey information as through our telephones. The reason is that photons have no mass, and thus can travel at the speed of light. It is now established that our brains produce *biophotons*, hence can convey information much faster than an electric current.

In addition to that, there is the *quantum tunneling*, which would account for instantaneous communication. The wonders will never cease! And we are just beginning to scratch the surface. The scientists still study rats' brains in the hope of learning something about our own biological computers. Our brains.

Maybe they are thinking only of themselves.

Thank God (Universe? Omnipresent Consciousness?) that as energy we appear to be immortal. Or, at least, our Consciousness is. On the other hand, as I mentioned in *DELUSIONS*, according to the British science historian James Burke: *"Evolution advances at somewhere between dead slow and dead slow."*

One day we shall learn that by killing others we are killing integral parts of ourselves. After all, there is but One Omnipresent Consciousness that individualizes Itself in all of us. Hence, we are One. And this applies to all fauna and flora. Wherever life manifests Itself.

Yet, for now, in the kindergarten, we appear to enjoy killing. Not just to eat but for fun. Ask any dictator. Or aspiring dictator. Or trophy hunter.

We are still very, very, very primitive species.

Perhaps we ought to start from scratch?
In *DELUSIONS* I proposed to get:

"a dozen imaginary deep bathtubs, with a dozen volunteers, preferably theoretical physicists, who will submerge themselves in the imaginary warm water, relax, and dream up a new universe which makes sense. The new universe, imaginary or not, would have a reality based on quanta of light. With the incredible diversity of waves at their disposal, they could build our bodies, in their imagination, spanning light-years, or shrinking us to enter and examine an atom from the inside, dodging a cloud of electrons whirling all around us. Wouldn't that be fun?"

I thought that we might give them a chance. After all, for theoretical physicists anything is possible. That's why they are theoretical. Practice is an entirely different story. Given them enough time and enough hot water in their tubs, and their 'biophotos' will generate enough ideas, and spread them throughout the present Universe through 'biophotonic' quantum entanglement, for us to enjoy new freedom of communication if not instantaneous travel.

I only mention this to illustrate just one possibility for our future. As for our biologists, they needn't worry. They'll assume titles of 'photologists' and keep evolving as if nothing has happened.

Ain't we got fun?

~~~~

For the rest of the POSTCRIPTUM, I shall reprint an *updated* version of the rest of my thoughts expressed in *DELUSIONS*. After all, they are already imaginary conclusions, hence, with a few additions, belong as much here as there. If you've already read them, and have no desire to stay up to date, please move on to the APPENDIX I - THE PRESENT.

And now for a moment of folly, or... a word about the electromagnetic spectrum. With the scientists assuring us that the universe consists principally of empty space, let us examine the range of energies that inhabit this abysmal emptiness.

The electromagnetic spectrum is traditionally divided into regions of radio waves, microwaves, infrared radiation, visible light, ultraviolet rays, X-rays, and gamma rays. I'm sure we shall soon discover a dozen others. (Not to mention neutrinos, which might not have any mass either. They seem to go through mass without even slowing down.)

The entire range of radiation extending in frequency from approximately 10^{23} hertz to 0 hertz or, in corresponding wavelengths, from 10^{-13} centimeters to infinity and including, in order of decreasing frequency, cosmic-ray photons, gamma rays, x-rays, ultraviolet radiation, visible light, infrared radiation, microwaves, and radio waves. I am offering the abundance of numbers only to illustrate how much more flexibility we would have with a reality build on photons, than we have at present with reality built on atoms.

Visible light has a wavelength shorter than the size of a bacterium. Radio waves can be as short as a millimeter, or be as many as, say, 30,000 kilometers long. Really! They are very long compared to the rest of the electromagnetic spectrum. The radio spectrum is divided into a number of 'bands' based on their wavelength and usability for communication purposes. They extend from the Very Low Frequency portion of the spectrum through the Low, Medium, High, Very High, Ultra High, and Super High to the Extra High Frequency range. Above the EHF band comes infrared radiation and *only then* visible light.

I think I'd like to have my body constructed from quanta of radio waves. The whole range. (Forget, for now, my photonic proposal. That would be a later evolutionary prospect.)

Why not?

I'd be detectible, and be able to detect my surroundings for miles, so to speak, as well as squeeze my prongs into very tiny crevices.

There are other options, of course. Gamma rays are generated by nuclear reactions (*e.g.,* radioactive decay). At first sight, not much use for those in my "photonology"; yet, they do exhibit some interesting aspects.

Astronomers have spotted gamma ray emissions coming from the Crab Pulsar at far higher energies than expected. Within the nebula lies the Crab Pulsar—a tiny, rapidly spinning neutron star that sprays highly energetic electromagnetic rays out at its poles like a lighthouse beam, sweeping past the Earth 30 times a second. The pulsar's enormous magnetic field is known to gather up particles and accelerate them—in a process much like particle accelerators here on Earth. As those particles move in curved paths, they emit the gamma rays that we can measure. OK. Maybe we could use some of them. We could give them a spin. Being made up of gamma rays would give us enormous power. The scientists found emissions at more than 100 gigaelectronvolts—100 billion times more energetic than visible light.

Just think of that for a moment...

Now, that's quite a range of characteristics to choose from. You can confirm some of the data at http://www.sciencemag.org and other Internet sources. Some I researched elsewhere. As Shakespeare said, all the world's a stage—my stage. Think of a theater where actors are made up of photons. All sorts of photons. A little like holographic projections, only real.

Why all this data?

To stimulate the minds of the theoretical astrophysicists in their bathtubs. Or anyone else who takes regular baths.

I will leave you with a poser.

Since we know that neither we, nor the Universe is 'solid', and the incredibly diverse spectrum of energy inhabits the whole of the Universe, and that energy has characteristics of both, waves and quanta, what if our true nature were to be made up of light? What I am suggesting is that, perhaps, it already is, only we can't see most of it.

We could be made up of quanta (not subatomic particles that are essentially empty space, but units or quanta of photons) with wavelengths spanning from submicroscopic all the way to infinity. A little like gods. A lot like gods? To quote Sir Isaac Newton:

> *"Are not gross Bodies and Light convertible into one another, ...and may not Bodies receive much of their Activity from the Particles of Light which enter their Composition?"*

Was Isaac Newton a scientist or a prophet?
Both, you say?
You may be right!

As for the atheists, it is a matter of unparalleled indifference to me whether they are theists, deists, agnostics or atheists. What matters to me is what effect their personal beliefs have on their behaviour and relationship to other people, animals, all living matter and reality in general. There are ample examples of animals acting towards members of *other* species with compassion comparative to that which we, humans, do when seeing our own species in trouble. Most of us tend to ignore members of other species needing our help. At best we often shoot them to put them out of their misery. Or their state of happiness? The more primitive members of the human species still collect animal trophies.

Other species don't.

Well, those more advanced amongst them—those not endowed with the Dawkins' *Selfish Gene* to the exclusion of all others. Nevertheless, members of various species have been observed helping members of other species, not just those with which they share their a little less-selfish gene.

On the other hand, CSN News.com reports:

> *"A new analysis from Georgetown University that attempts to document the economic value of religion in U.S. society found that **the faith sector is worth $1.2 trillion, more than the combined revenue of the top 10 technology companies in the country, including Apple, Amazon, and Google.**"*

Makes me wonder if one shouldn't become a bishop, or a priest, or at least a preacher... let alone an evangelist!

However, if I understand the evolutionary biologists correctly, they contrive to assign all the goodness, morality, decency, empathy, pity, and of course altruism, exclusively to the "selfish gene", with possible fringe assistance from the memes. They also introduce a concept new to me: that of "reciprocal altruism".

Now that's as good an oxymoron as any I've ever heard—although I have heard it said that altruism is not a quality but an act of self-preservation. Nevertheless, an act performed with the sole purpose of what one might receive in return is not altruism at all.

It is trade, often selfish, at that.

But to confuse the behaviour known as the Potlatch Effect—wherein one gives only to exhibit one's superiority over the recipient of one's gift—with altruism, as anything but an aberration of ego, is truly a perversion in itself. I am sure there are such humans around, and not just rival chieftains in the Pacific Northwest; but they are as low on the evolutionary scale as a university professor who expects to be accorded respect for having awarded his or her student an undeservedly high mark to raise his own reputation of achievement.

Yes, I have met such people. Such 'professors'.

Edgar Cayce, the late American psychic (an attribute or ability dismissed by most biologists), once said that there is only one sin, and that is self. I suspect he was referring to our ego, not our Higher Self. And I suspect he intended the word 'sin' in its original sense, *i.e., "missing the mark of being human"*. Or was it of being constructed in the image of god?

Now, I do not object to biologists deifying the gene as the exclusive source of all goodness and altruistic impulses in us, animals, provided they will allot equal measure to our propensity towards murder and mayhem, and to the joy we derive from killing just for fun (as all the hunters will affirm), and to the distinguished scientists who spend half their lives attempting to design and build weapons of mass destruction. I can only assume that the highly altruistic gene is no longer just selfish and, indeed, has evolved into a seed of evil, whatever the biologists understand by this word.

I am not sure how such untrammeled biological diversity fits into Pragmatic Realism, let alone Pragmatic Reality; but, it seems to me, it makes as much sense as being made up of empty space. If so, then the scientists don't really have to make up any of their theories. Perhaps they, too, are filled with empty space—both the scientists and their theories. We seem to make up reality as we go along. Beauty, common sense, even truth, as well as the characteristics of a gene, are in the eyes of the beholder.

On January 22nd, 2017, we heard the *U.S. Counselor to the President*, (during a Meet the Press interview), use an unusual phrase: *"Alternative facts"*. I must assume that the speaker suffered from a distorted sense of humour. Perhaps she was speaking about some empty space?

As for the diverse energies, they continue to exist without our conscious assistance and, after all, as the Preacher in Ecclesiastes 1:1-3 affirms, *"There is nothing new under the sun."* This same Preacher also proclaims, emphatically, that all actions of man are inherently vain, futile, empty, meaningless, temporary, transitory, fleeting, or mere breath. Perhaps we inherited all these traits and abilities from the selfish gene?

On the other hand, the mystics of yore proposed millennia ago that we are all beings of light. Perhaps their time has come.

Light! Isn't this exactly what String Theory proposes? Does it not affirm that at the fundamental level everything consists of light and electricity? On the other hand, String Theory is already *passé*. What we now have is 5 String Theories. At least we had five, until Edward Witten, an American theoretical physicist and professor of mathematical physics at the Institute for Advanced Study in Princeton, New Jersey, compared by many to be today's Einstein, insisted that it's all just One Theory, only we are looking at it from 5 different points of view. And he called it the M Theory. Only no one knows what the M stands for.

You might well ask, "Who cares?"

Well, the scientists are deluding themselves again. Until they'll be able to test the theory, any theory, in a laboratory, even if it's the size of CERN—in part a ring 27 kilometers in circumference and employing some 4,000 physicists worldwide—it, the M, or any other theory, remains philosophy *not* science.

In the meantime, the scientists at CERN continue to waste our money. They finally discovered the Higgs boson which, they say, is a 'fundamental' particle. If we ignore the 'strings' and the ensuing theories, the Higgs boson is expected to be one of the basic building blocks of the Universe. It was also the last missing piece in the leading theory of particle physics—known as the Standard Model—which describes how particles and forces interact. Finding the Higgs was a key goal for the $10bn particle smasher. Just before the epic discovery of the boson, Prof. Stefan Soldner-Rembold, a senior scientist at CERN had this to say:

> *"The Higgs particle would, of course, be a great discovery, but it would be an even greater discovery if it didn't exist where theory predicts it to be."*

Just think. Something that no one ever saw, touched, smelled, heard, or tasted, with our five senses made up of mostly empty space, until recently not even detected with the multibillion-dollar technology, does actually exist. Wonders will never cease.

Back to the drawing board.
Nevertheless, they found it.[1] Particle colliders, detectors, and computers capable of looking for Higgs bosons took more than 30 years to develop, from around 1980 to 2012. Then someone said... *Eureka.*
Now what?
What the hell does *eureka* mean, they might have asked...
Let's give them another $10 billion and they'll look for something else. I suspect that there is only one condition. It must be invisible. As for the $10 billion of tax money, it still is but a tiny fraction of the $1.2 trillion spent on American faith. We are lucky that physicists are not religiously inclined.

On yet another hand, with the exception of the horrendous waste of money, *theoretical* physicists are much closer to my heart than many other 'all-knowing' scientists. I always said that Einstein was my favourite philosopher. But trust me, at the fundamental level, you and I are just light. And the infinite number of 'strings' all around us are playing an indescribable celestial symphony. Some call it *Musica Universalis*. When you'll hear it—you'll know. God will be the conductor. And then, when you look closer at the Maestro's features, you'll recognize your own face.

~~~

(1) "A new particle with a mass of 125 GeV was discovered in 2012 and later confirmed to be the Higgs boson with more precise measurements. The Higgs boson is an elementary particle in the Standard Model of particle physics, produced by the quantum excitation of the Higgs field, one of the fields in particle physics theory."

(Higgs boson, Wikipedia)

APPENDIX I
THE PRESENT
(The Church)
Including CUSTODIANS OF CULTURE

> *"Love one another."*
> **John 13:34 (KJV)**

> *"The distinction between the past, present and future is only a stubbornly persistent illusion."*
> **Albert Einstein (1879 - 1955)**

> *"In rivers, the water that you touch is the last of what has passed and the first of that which comes; so with present time."*
> **Leonardo da Vinci (1452 - 1519)**
> Painter, draftsman, sculptor, architect, and engineer

Learning to love one another was our instruction during the previous Zodiac Age of Pisces. Not that we must stop practicing love now, in the New Age, but if we've learned our lesson, we shall continue enhancing the Universe. If not, then there is a good chance that we, or at least our Egos, will be recycled in a friendly, nearby neighborhood, Black Hole. All is energy, remember? And no one yet is known to have escaped the fatal attraction of a Black Hole.

You might still make it.

I mean evade the fatal attraction.

After all, time is a dimension of the phenomenal world. Your Being abides in the eternal Now. It might consider you worth saving. You and your Ego.

And, after all, the energy of Love makes us ONE.

In the humdrum of keeping our bodies alive, here is a single secret that people appear to forget.

~~~ WE ARE NOT OUR BODIES ~~~

We live within them, we enjoy our Becoming within them, but we also do so in our homes, our automobiles—all our possessions which enhance our physical pleasures.

And pleasures they are intended to be. After all, we are said to be children of a Magnanimous Deity that sculpted us out of clay and placed us in a beautiful Garden purely for our pleasure. It's a nice story. It's all symbolic, of course. The Garden is still there. Or here. Waiting for us to enjoy it. It is our state of Consciousness. Our awareness of life. Limited for now, but imbued with infinite potential, all for our pleasure.

Yet there, in that garden of our Consciousness, we started thinking that knowledge of the phenomenal Universe is more important than the joy of Becoming. We confused the consciousness generated by our brain with the Omnipresent Consciousness that created us, and which remains our true nature. We confuse the Effect with the Cause.

It's such a pity...

We keep forgetting that only our Being is eternal, while our Becoming is transient. That's all. That is our sole mistake. We are forgetting that we are immortal, indestructible, extremely powerful individualizations of the Omnipresent Creative Energy that our forefathers called Spirit. Yet knowledge and acceptance of this fact alone would influence our thoughts, our emotions, our actions, and the way we feel and enjoy our Becoming.

So what is the purpose of Becoming?

What is the purpose of Life?

We are the Creators of diversity in the phenomenal

Universe—in the Universe that changes in every imaginable way every second... and yet, until Einstein spoiled our fun, we called it real.

We seem to forget that as Beings we are also immortal observers of the Process of Becoming. As Beings we inspire the elements of the phenomenal Universe to continue becoming more beautiful, more enchanting, such as even the Paradise would pale next to its beauty. The Potential is infinite, and so is our ability to translate it into our transient reality.

Why transient?

Because the ability to enhance it still further is infinite. So why settle for second best? No matter how beautiful it already is, it is but the first step of the reality we can create during the rest of eternity.

Did you ever see the kaleidoscope of colours that adorn fish in the depth of the ocean? Did you stop to admire the patterns that enhance birds, butterflies, or even bugs which you might have stepped on accidentally?

They are all gratuitous presents derived from our Being created for the sole purpose of enhancing our lives, our Becoming. All we need do is to add to their beauty. After all, Being and Becoming are inseparable. They are One... They are the two aspects of our nature.

Being without Becoming is like a great artist who has no canvas, no paint, no brushes to create immortal works of art. Becoming without Being is like having all the equipment but no talent, no inspiration, no idea what and how to transfer anything onto the canvas.

Yes, the two must be One.

Yet, the separation of these two aspects of our nature is so very evident in this day and age. Think of the great composers of the past and compare their creations with the noise that accompanies most of the pseudo art that fills our

TV screens. Of course there are exceptions, but in most cases the inspiration seems limited to making money, not to enhance our Becoming.

Hence, the Age of Aquarius.

The *Few* of the past have exhausted their talents. Those among the *Many* who heard the inner voice, have become corrupted by the power it had given them. Hence now, seemingly in desperation, the Universe opens it floodgates to the "Third Party".

To reiterate...

The Great Exceptions of the past, perhaps in their final reincarnation in our reality, are gone. Then the many, probably the creators of the so-called Democracy, which was intended to open the gates of creativity to the Many, have met an untimely demise. Those who are leaders of the democratic principles who still fill the houses of parliaments, of senates and other groups pretending to serve people, have become dismally corrupt. They filled their pockets with money at the expense of the "Third Party", of the masses.

And now Zodiac says NO MORE!

The Age of Aquarius will return the power to ordinary men and women whose ability to influence their future will be greatly multiplied.

Yet, everything has its price.

While the diversity produced by billions of people will grow exponentially from which the Universe will select fragments of enhancement, it will be balanced by times of anarchy, that will cleanse the corruption of the past Age. The paradox of this transition is that only the Few will realize that our physical bodies, the embodiments of our Consciousness of Being, always were and continue to be transient. In fact, illusory. The seeming incongruity of this phase of Becoming is that our embodiments are and always were transient. Hence eradication of the Ego that accompanies them benefits the Being that inhabited Its temporary phenomenal enclosure.

Don't get me wrong. Our bodies are most wondrous miracles of biological engineering. Who knows how many billions of years it took to make them. No, not just here on Earth, but throughout the eternal Universe. And they will continue to be as prodigious the next time round. As is each phase of the ever-changing phenomenal Universe.

After all, the Creative Energy of Becoming manifests through the miracle of metamorphosis. Ever improving, ever more enchanting, ever replenishing the breathtaking beauty of the phenomenal Universe.

Please, join the Few in your calling. The power is within you. Every single one of you.

Ye are gods!

CUSTODIANS OF CULTURE

> Below an updated excerpt from *Essay # 18*,
> *Beyond Religion vol. III*,
> previously published in *DELUSIONS*.
> Anyone who already read it in *DELUSIONS*
> or the original version,
> please move on to **Appendix II**.
> (Or, enjoy it once more!)

Sometime ago, a dear friend of mine, having read a number of my essays, suggested that, on occasion, he had an impression that I have it 'in' for the Church. Particularly, the Roman Church. He was very polite about it, but, "Well," he said, "you don't seem to find much good to say about Holy Mother Church."

What could I say? I don't.

Not much.

Not as long as the Church, the Holy Roman Catholic

and Apostolic Church, takes it upon herself to speak on matters pertaining to the teaching of Christ. For try as I might, each time I attempted to reconcile Christ's teaching with the Church's manifest philosophy, I have been reminded of a man who asked: *"Master, what good thing shall I do, that I may have eternal life?"* And after a preliminary discussion the answer came loud and clear: *"...go and sell that thou hast, and give to the poor, and thou shall have treasure in heaven: and come and follow me."*

The last 2,000 years have made it abundantly clear that the Church has absolutely no interest in any treasures in Heaven. On the other hand, the brazen agglomeration of priceless wealth, which I suspect exceeds even that of the British Empire, (which R. Buckminster Fuller once called:

"...history's most successful world-outlaw organization..."

leaves me full of admiration. However, since the Church wouldn't follow the Christ, I could hardly be expected to follow the Church.

But this is true *only* of the area of my particular interest: The area of *Inquiry into the Nature of Being*. My personal inquiry into the legacy of past Masters, which to this day appears to remain obscure, enigmatic, full of mystery, to all but a few members of the Church I'd ever met.

Perhaps I should meet more people.

On the other hand, I have nothing but admiration and undying gratitude to the Church, present and past, in many other areas that are *almost* as dear to me. I wish my readers, and particularly my friend, to know that I hold the Church responsible for my countless moments of joy, of visual, aural and tactile pleasure that contribute greatly to the fabric of my daily life. In fact, outside my marriage, no other organization has contributed so abundantly to the pleasure of my senses as the Church.

So... isn't the Church enhancing the Universe?
The phenomenal, illusory Universe...
Let me count the ways.

I held my breath as I entered the Basilica of Saint Peter. What magnificent space, what resplendent vistas! I dare anyone, of any faith or religion, not to derive pleasure, not to admire the euphoric splendor (spiritual decadence only if you are a spoilsport) of the central building of the Church. The sensuously polished marbles, the forests of columns—forthright and upright, soaring towards heavenly domes, or multihued and spiral, mysterious... filled me with awe. The armies of sculptured saints, the galleries of paintings of more saintly figures, all immortalized right here, on Earth, for posterity.

The greatest names of the 16th century, Bramante, Michelangelo and Raphael, have been mustered to contribute their genius to this monument of human endeavour. And all this thanks to but one man, Pope Julius II. Admittedly there are those who call his reign *"the decadence of papacy"*, but there is another way of looking at this period. Without Julius, St. Peter would never have happened.

And then there is the Sistine Chapel ceiling, the papal apartments, the papal portrait galleries, the inexhaustible works of art in the Vatican Museum, the consummate splendor of other Vatican buildings, the gardens... and, last but not least, the superb archives of the Vatican library...

Who else could provide us with such unprecedented riches?

And this is just the headquarters.

Wherever I went, wherever I travelled, in Europe, in Africa, in the North, Central or South America, everywhere, in every country, my joy was multiplied by the sheer number of beautiful churches, often amassing the best art and architecture that money could buy of local and imported talent... Often of genius left unknown, forgotten in small

Brazilian, Mexican, Peruvian towns, in neglected English villages, in small hamlets the world over. The Gothic style alone could not have been inspired by any authority other than that of the Church. The Early English, the Decorated, the Curvilinear or Flamboyant, the sedate more reserved Tudor, all testify to the Church reaching ever higher, yet ever more lugubriously, for something she, the church, seems to have lost.

But for me, for my own pleasure, the heritage speaks of nothing but beauty, of human endeavour, of the creative spirit.

Yes, the Church was enhancing the Universe.

And then, by unmitigated contrast, I saw the inspiring, flowing, soaring effects of Amiens and other ecclesiastic monuments of the great French Cathedral cities... high towers, pinnacles, superabundant sculpture, effervescent stained glass, filtering preternatural light to the streamlined interiors. Wherever the Church stretched her mighty arms, she left an indelible mark of beauty in her prodigious wake.

And then there is the music.

I defy anyone to point to any other source as abundant as the Church in commanding composers to produce their best for the good of all. Music cannot be retained by those who commissioned its fervor. It is a free gift to all who would listen. From the *aria antiqua*, through the doleful canticles to the Ambrosian and Gregorian chants, echoing among the stone walls of ancient monasteries, to Handel's Messiah and other Oratorios. And who could claim that Bach wasn't first and foremost a church's composer?

And then we find Tosca's incomparable *Vissi d'arte*, Desdemona's plaintive *Ave Maria*, Elizabeth de Valois's *Tu che le vanita conoscesti,* and so many other sublime arias all, surely, inspired by the Church's teaching.

And finally there is Mozart who, through his ecstatic prodigious and ebullient *Requiem,* allowed us a peak into his personal heaven. Could any of these have been born without the Church's influence?

I think not.

And there is more—much more...

So I am to this day, and intend to remain, grateful to the Holy Mother, the Church. Grateful for her past inspiration and for giving access to us all, today, to share in her splendid, unequal aegis. And to those who belittle her wealth, I can only ask: Who else is prepared to spend millions, countless millions, on the maintenance of such legacy?

Perhaps this fact alone is the greatest blessing. The Church is assuring that the wonder of human creativity will remain accessible not only to us but also to our children's children. Who says the Church cannot serve two masters? Perhaps we should forgive and forget the preacher's peccadilloes and be grateful for his obvious achievements. By standing on guard of such illustrious past, perhaps the Church might also inspire our distant future.

And, after all, the future is our own.

APPENDIX II
THE ESSENCE OF DIVERSITY
(Science)

> *"It is important to foster individuality for only the individual can produce the new ideas."*
> **Albert Einstein (1879 - 1955)**

> *"It is time for parents to teach young people early on that in diversity there is beauty and there is strength."*
> **Maya Angelou (1928 - 2014)**
> African-American poet, singer, memoirist

> *"Isn't it amazing that we are all made in God's image, and yet there is so much diversity among his people?"*
> **Desmond Tutu**
> 1984 Nobel Prize for Peace

The need for DIVERSITY alone explains the need for the Age of Aquarius. No matter how bad, innocuous, or even destructive ideas we generate, they are all passed through the sieve of the "Final Judgment" of the *Event Horizon*, before being incorporated into the matrix of the phenomenal Universe. The ideas that cannot sustain their phenomenal presence in the reality of balance, fall into the Black Holes and become recycled to reenter and seminate the evolutionary cycle as pure energy of Consciousness.

This judgment is not presided over by a high court, only by the consequences such ideas have on the phenomenal Universe. A bomb is just an innocent word until it is dropped from an unthinking, primitive pilot, completely ignoring the damage the bomb will create.

Yet, even then, the moment he returns from his 'heroic'

mission of killing people from 33,000 feet, he might suffer from post-traumatic stress disorder, the so-called PTSD. Many veterans who never heard about such a condition will fall under its spell. It is not a punishment imposed by an unforgiving deity, but a question of cause and effect. That's all. The ancients called it *Karma*.

On September 27, 2019, *The* Guardian[1] offered the following report:

> *"The army, navy and marines all saw the rate of suicides go up this year, with ... US military suicides surged this year to a record high among active duty..."*

Wikipedia adds:

> **"United States military veteran suicide** *is an ongoing phenomenon regarding a reportedly high rate of suicide among U.S. military* **veterans**, *in comparison to the general public. According to the most recent report published by the United* **States Department of Veterans Affairs** *(VA) in 2016, which analyzed 55 million veterans' records from 1979 to 2014, the current analysis indicates that an average of 20 veterans a day die from suicide."*

That's only a fraction of the 3,287 who die daily in road accidents, or the 46 per day out of a total population of 330 million who are murdered daily, but it does indicate the malaise of the nation. Of course a number of those deaths might also have been veterans.

However we regard it, the Universal Laws will not be broken. *Karma* will not be denied. It is quite impersonal, regardless what Washington or the Pentagon might say. What I find amazing is that the government of the US, which has all these data, does not seem to draw any conclusions from them. And what I find even more astounding is the sheer number of veterans.

55,000,000 from 1979 to 2014. This is more than the total population of all but five European countries.

Incredible!

It seems that nothing is free or indifferent in this world. Everything has its consequences. No punishments, no awards, although medals might be pinned to the heroic chests of the veterans. Just consequences. These are unavoidable, or as Isaac Newton would have said, they are the Cause and Effect, regardless of what politicians, scientists, or religious leaders might say.

Karma rules supreme.

Yet even when we swallow our shock of seeing the dismal numbers denying the suffering of the US veterans, they pale when compared to the inhumanity of World Wars.

Once again, Wikipedia reports that the total number of military and civilian casualties in World War I was about 40 million: with 20 million dead and about the same number of the military personnel wounded.

Yet even these incredible figures pale when compared to the next global massacre. According to "**World War II** casualties - Wikipedia", between 1939 and 1945:

> "***Deaths*** *directly caused by the war (including military and civilians **killed**) are estimated at 50–56 million people, while there were an additional estimated 19 to 28 million **deaths** from war-related disease and famine. Civilian **deaths** totaled 50-55 million."*

Other sources, also on the Internet, report that some 75

CONCLUSIONS

million people, about 3% of the 1940 world population (est. 2.3 billion), *died in World War II*, including about 20 million military personnel and *40 million civilians,* many of whom died because of deliberate genocide, massacres, mass bombings, disease, and starvation.

This probably does not include the deaths of politicians who may have kicked the bucket due to overeating and drinking while celebrating victories.

I am a Canadian, living in the shadow of the most powerful country in the world. They have already achieved this distinction. However, to assure their capability to continue killing:

> *"On September 28, 2018, Trump signed the Department of Defense appropriations bill. The approved 2019 Department of Defense discretionary budget is* **$686.1 billion***. It has also been described as '$617 billion for the base budget and another $69 billion for war funding'."*

Trump is their president. The head honcho. This budget is 10 times bigger, in the US, than their budget for *education* which is limited to *$68 billion.*

This does prove conclusively, however, that the human species is on a downward spiral, falling at an astonishing speed in both our murderous instincts and stupidity. Whatever other diversities we may have introduced in the same period of time, the art of indiscriminate murder must surely stand well ahead of all others. We must face the fact that we are a species of killers.

And our instincts are not limited to just killing each other. In the United States alone, more than 100 million *animals* are reported *killed by hunters* each year. To that proud number we must add, *inter alia*, Lions, Leopards, Buffalo, Black Rhino, White Rhino, and Crocodiles, which are hunted, also *inter alia,* in Tanzania, Botswana, South Africa, Zimbabwe, Zambia, and Mozambique, not to mention the rest of the world.

To stress how depraved we have become, I've counted at least 15 *World Hunting Awards.* According to Wikipedia, the Major Awards are distributed at the SCI Annual Hunters' Convention at the Night of the Hunter. These are proudly awarded for the killers who can prove a requisite number of murders.

We are killers, and apparently we love killing.

Karma will take care of that. Guaranteed.

And yet, the Universe demands of us diversity. Not just in behaviour or philosophy, but, perhaps, by discarding previous beliefs to make room for new ones. Perhaps we ought to think long and hard before we offer diversity at the expense of other people. At the expense of other embodiments of the Immortal Consciousness. Perhaps we can destroy only that which we, ourselves, have created.

All the rest is off our limits.

And this brings us to the problem raised in *DELUSIONS*—Appendix II, previously entitled **Science**. As science deals only with the phenomenal reality, we must include its aspects, no matter how transient they might be, in the totality of Becoming.

What I have in mind is the question of where our artificial intelligence might take us.

As we know, no matter how very misunderstood the concept, religions insisted—indeed, continue to insist—that we are created in the image of God. They failed to tell us what do they mean by God, which is hardly surprising, since they insist on reversing the order of creation and, instead, invented a god in our image.

Once we reject the concept of a God in our image, we open the whole Universe to our imagination. But most of all, we become amenable to Einstein's maxim that *all is energy*. This, surely, would include God and other gods, be they in any image, or even before their images had been formed in our illusory reality.

Yet, if we were so generous in the allotment of choices for a multitude of divinities, then we have no choice but to accept the threat that Ray Kurzweil may have a point. His theory, that artificial intelligence of robots might match if not exceed ours, is expressed in his book *The Singularity is Near* (Viking, Penguin Group). His concepts are further discussed in Appendix III, below. Enough said that our creativity may transcend biology. After all, the Universe is said to be *stranger than we can imagine.*

There is yet another question that fluctuates in my mind. If magnificent non-biological robots exceed our, *i.e.,* human capabilities, will it be as unreal, as illusory as the rest of our reality? Will it be just an illusion?

How I wish that Albert were still with us. We would have been able to ask him that.

I suspect, he'd just smile.

~~~

(1) www.theguardian.com

APPENDIX III
THE INCONVENIENT TRUTH
(Richard Dawkins)

> *"Science without religion is lame,*
> *religion without science is blind."*
> *"A person starts to live when he can live outside himself."*
> **Albert Einstein (1879 - 1955)**
> Nobel Prize in Physics in 1921

> *"Science is the belief in the ignorance of experts."*
> *"I would rather have questions that can't be answered than answers*
> *that can't be questioned."*
> **Richard Feynman (1918 - 1988)**
> American physicist,
> recipient of joint Nobel Prize in Physics in 1965

> *"Let us try to teach generosity and altruism,*
> *because we are born selfish."*
> **Richard Dawkins PhD, atheist**

Religions hold that there is a God in Heaven to which we might aspire to go once we die. Apparently we are to go there, disembodied, and do absolutely nothing forever and ever. Forever after.

Now that's quite a long time for doing nothing...

Even if disembodied...

Yeshûa placed this Heaven within us, here and now. They can't both be right. Scientists might accept a God as Creative Energy. But now—following the String Theory, or at least the M-theory[1], which postulates, or at least suggests, that the Universe might be eternal—there may have been, and continues to be, ample time to evolve a whole pantheon of Gods that would populate not only our Earth, but innumerable galaxies adorning our night sky.

Let's face it. It is all a very Inconvenient Truth.

To deny such a possibility is to place limitations on our evolution. Considering that we have most probably evolved from microorganism hugging the periphery of deep-ocean vents, the next upward step is more than probable. Even our myths spread across the whole Earth attest to that.

However, what we must bear in mind is that diversity appears to demand a cyclic movement. All nature appears to sustain itself in repetitive cycles. On Earth this manifests in seasons, but I suspect that our Earth reflects a universal order that is proven to work. Until we discover what those cycles are, what causes them, we are subject to their fluctuations.

No matter, history strongly suggests that there had been individuals who gave evidence of quite unprecedented potential, which, according to them, rests within us all. Be they gods of our myths, artists whose works have become immortal, or mystics on whose teaching (if grossly misunderstood) religions have grown, the evidence is there. After all, there had always been the (very) *Few*, who emerged from the "*Many that were Called*". All of them point to our future potential.

And then, there is science.

Science does not accept the existence of Heaven. (Obviously, no scientist had ever held a beautiful woman in his arms. Nor had she never felt lost in his. And this is only the antechamber of Paradise.)

No matter. Heaven is a state of Consciousness.

Science also does not concern itself with our potential. Its only purpose is to understand and exploit what already is manifested in the phenomenal reality. It attempts to explain where evolution has brought us to this day. The *eurekas* of science discover what may have been around for thousands of years. Science does not create, it only exploits—although it has also been described as a method that enables us to understand the world we live in.

Nevertheless, science takes care of survival of the vast majority of people from whose ranks, often unpredictably, the Few emerge. The rest benefit from the perspicacity of quite many who, while having heard of the wondrous possibilities fermenting within them, are not yet ready to take the next step. What stops them is, regrettably, their Ego which, as we know, is generated by the artificial intelligence of our brain or, perhaps also, by our neurological and endocrinal systems.[3]

The only consolations, though not for the vast majority of scientists, is that in spite of the doctorships they award themselves as evidence of their expertise, the reality of their study is not real. Even Einstein, who surely must be included in the ranks of the Few, defined our phenomenal worlds as unreal. As illusion. Perhaps, one day, other scientists will follow in his illustrious footsteps.

Alas, there are always only a Few.

The very few...

And among the select Few we must include the theoretical physicist Richard Phillips Feynman.

He defined science quite clearly.

It is, he said, *"... the belief in the ignorance of experts."* This sentiment might be unfair to the Few, but it certainly rings true for the experts of the Flat Earth Society, as well as true of the thousands of scientists from the ranks of the Many, let alone the Third Party.

And this is the crux of the matter.

The Few come from *all* ranks of humanity. They are not defined by the degrees they might have, nor by social, economic, academic, or any other position they might hold. The Few can be found amongst the Many as well as amongst the Third Party. They join the select Few when they awaken to the Truth. When they realize that the world we live in is an illusion, an ephemeral transitional reality that changes by metamorphosis of the rate of vibrations of the Omnipresent Energy.

But most of all, they emerge from the tiny group of people who are convinced that they are individualizations of the Omnipresent Creative Energy of Consciousness. Although, more often than not, they'd never admit it in public.

That's about it.

What remains is merely the acceptance of the eternal Now. The acceptance of the Energy of Being that metamorphoses on a continuous basis into the energy of Becoming. Hence, nothing phenomenal is, or at least remains for very long, as real. It is in constant, unavoidable state or metamorphosis.

This is as much true of our physical bodies, as of the whole Universe. Physically, we, and everything around us, are in a state of flux.

You no longer inhabit the body you occupied a second ago. What you thought you were no longer exists, although all that you could ever be already exists in its potential state of Being.

Or even, perhaps, in the phenomenal Quantum Field?

Let me know if you find out.

There is one aspect of the omnipresence of the Creative Energy of Consciousness (sometimes referred to as God) that is often misunderstood. Omnipresence implies that the Consciousness is present within and without everyone and everything. Not just within humanity, or any other living creatures, but within and without all things. It is present within every cell of your body, every microbe, every atom and subatomic particle. Its presence is what gives every fragment of the phenomenal reality its character, its mode of behaviour, its beauty and its purpose. Likewise, even while it is present within everyone and everything, everyone and everything exists within It.[2]

This is the true meaning of Oneness.

The consequence of this fact is that every single item, live or inert, already is programmed with the function it is intended to perform. We have a choice to assist in the fulfillment of such functions or, using our artificial intelligence which (regrettably?) can act independently of its intended destiny, enhance various functions by increasing the diversity of their destiny. This is why it is of vital importance for each one of us to discover our purpose. Our intended destiny. If we don't, then... as with all actions in the phenomenal reality, there are consequences.

Although I found it vaguely inconvenient, I raised the question in Appendix II, above, whether a robot of human invention might exceed human capabilities.

Well, there is an inconvenient problem.

Once again, referring to Einstein, anything or anybody in the phenomenal reality would remain as unreal, as illusory, as we are; and if so, what would be its aspect of Being. Wouldn't its creative force be the human artificial intelligence, which, after all, is as transient and illusory as the product it creates? A sort of illusory god, as most human gods are?

But what is even more important, at least to me, is the question whether such a robot could exceed not only our present abilities but our ultimate phenomenal potential?

To repeat Ray Kurzweil's *The Singularity Is Near: When Humans Transcend Biology* is a 2005 non-fiction book about artificial intelligence and the proposed or imagined future of humanity. It is so described in Wikipedia. The problem I have with such a postulate is the transiency of our reality.

As for our, human abilities, there are things we shall do that our parents haven't even dreamt of, although there is some evidence that they have been known to our distant forefathers.
For instance, *quantum tunneling.*

This is my personal favourite. I liked it so much that I wrote a novel about it entitled *WALL*, and subtitled it (for the sake of marketing): *Love, Sex and Immortality.* This is a feature of quantum mechanics that allows objects to pass through barriers (walls, in my case) that should be impenetrable according to Newton's classical laws of physics. Forgive me for plugging my novel, but I'm sure that if you enjoy this book, or even if you don't (ha, ha), you'll enjoy the novel even more. Or to use *quantum language* (I just invented this term!), there is a strong probability that you might...

Apparently, there is so much empty space within each atom that, provided we align the atomic structure within the structure of the object through which it is intended to pass, the rest is easy. While this seems to be impossible from the mechanical point of view, it might be no more difficult than the countless miracles recorded in countless documents in the annals of human history.

Or... perhaps, Kurzweil's robots will do it.

As mentioned above, there are echoes of such feats as walking through walls, or walking on water, in ancient history. To take them seriously, we must again dismiss any notions that the scriptures are a religious document. All writings, in all parts of our history, describe the reality those people lived in, or the reality they imagined as real.

I'm not sure there is a difference.

So how did Yeshûa walk through a closed door? Or walk on water? Or convert water into wine? Or did the countless 'miracles' attributed to Father (Saint) Pio of Pietrelcina occur, including most incomprehensible healings and repeated bilocations? There were many...

We call them miracles.

I will, once again in harmony with Einstein, repeat his words:

"There are only two ways to live your life. One is as though nothing is a miracle. The other is as though everything is a miracle."

If you can create a multi-hued bird, or an elephant, or a fly or flee, then none of them would be miracles. After all, science dismisses miracles. They are not real, the scientists say.

They are an illusion, they affirm.

Well, apparently so may have been the "pre-miracle" conditions. And... so are the scientists?

And this is where, once again, Einstein comes in. We must decide how real are our illusions. This is not a new religion. Deeds performed by Father Pio were observable facts, witnessed by many, who look at them without mental cataracts obscuring their vision. The same I hold to be true of the countless 'miracles' performed by countless saints or mystics, let alone by Yeshûa at the onset of Christianity.

We have been descending into materiality ever since.

We should, however, never forget that the word 'saint' implies holiness, and the word holy means no more than 'whole' or 'complete'. It is a state of consciousness wherein the energies of Being and Becoming, even if just momentarily, became united. Became One.

That, strangely enough, is all there is to it!

Attempting to convert potential reality into an illusion of a materialistic vision, to regard it as real, is the greatest harm people can do to their own happiness. To their own fulfillment.

And yet, the vast majority do just that!

Perhaps we ought to start by trying to define the concept of a miracle. The most important aspect of a miracle is that it is *never* in opposition or denial of *Universal Laws*. In denial of nature. Of our reality. We've decided thousands of years ago that this cannot be done.

Remember Matthew? (see Chapter 12)

"...one jot or one tittle shall in no wise pass from the law..."

Not one tittle. Tittle is so small that it's not even included in most dictionaries! Denial of the Universal Laws would deny our reality. We would not exist. We would be no more. Nor would the Universe. There would be only the Eternal Potential, the Omnipresent Consciousness, in search for a way to express Itself.

When will humanity learn that *all* causes invariably originate in energy and not in "matter"? We, and no one else, create the illnesses on which the pharmaceutical and medical industries make good money. Illusions of illnesses?

The true reality is invariably perfect.

But we don't have to reject the truth. We are gods, remember. As I keep repeating, we and no one else creates our realities. As a child I had every imaginable disease that killed thousands of people. And now I don't. I don't have to react to negative energies generated by other people. In my reality, in my Paradise, there are no illnesses.

All we need do is find our passion and then enjoy it to the full. If we do so, the chances are that we shall become indispensable to the Universe. That we shall finally fulfill our purpose. That our contribution will enhance the reality we live in. That's what life is supposed to be about. That's what people do in Paradise. In the Heaven of their own creation.

Welcome to my world!

Yet there is more. Much more. The Singularity to which Kurzweil refers will not be achieved only by enormous progress in the non-biological artificial intelligence, but by reducing masses of people to the same status.

Our brains react to electromagnetic waves and thus we are strongly affected by our near-continuous exposure to electronic gadgetry, such as TV, tablets and telephones. The effects are still unpredictable. Although our scientists are not as yet sure if technology is destroying our brains, they strongly suspect that the radiation can trigger obsessive behaviour that can lead to depression.

> *"All day long, we're inundated by interruptions and alerts from our devices. Smartphones buzz to wake us up, emails stream into our inboxes, notifications from coworkers and far away friends bubble up on our screens, and "assistants" chime in with their own soulless voices."*
>
> Hilary Brueck
> Business Insider's "Your Brain on Apps".

Also, while the electronic devises increase our ability to reach conclusions requiring calculations, there is evidence that they slow down our inherent thinking processes.

Sooner or later we, humanity, must decide whether we want to improve our technology, or to improve our own abilities. If we make the wrong choice, we shall become inferior biological automatons, guided and controlled by our own creations.

As Kurzweil has said, *"Singularity is Near"*; only now, it carries disastrous connotations for humanity.

Also, as I have written in the prequel to *CONCLUSIONS*, according to science, which we cannot discard in the phenomenal reality:

> *"We must never forget that whatever we examine in physical world, that object is substantially if not completely changed at cellular and/or atomic level, before the examination is completed."*

And this fact has further connotations.
It is related to the (assumed) subliminal structure of the human mentality. As mentioned in METAMORPHOSIS, (Chapter 4), all new ideas, those not derived from previous experience, originate in our *unconscious*. No matter what peregrinations our mind makes, we cannot conceive of the *unconscious* inspiring a non-biological robot.

I'm willing to accept a limited *subconscious*, based on complex atomic structure, that would correspond to a magnificent computer memory storage, but not the *unconscious*, which is purely a non-phenomenal concept. It enables us, the *biological* robots, to compose music such as has never been heard before. It enables us to introduce diversity, which is the *sine qua non* aspect of our *raison d'être*.

Although there may be an infinite number of different biological structures, this fact alone will forever differentiate us from non-biological robots that, in my opinion, will vastly exceed human ability to derive knowledge from past experience, but will not result in adding originality to our reality.

Unless...

Unless Einstein and a few other select scientists are wrong. Personally, I doubt it. I strongly suspect Einstein and the select *Few* derived their (revolutionary) conclusions from their... *unconscious*. Most certainly not from their past experience.

For those who question non-phenomenal energies, allow me to list some of them. They are energies that have enormous influence on our action, behaviour, and even conceptualization of our reality, but cannot be measured by phenomenal (you can call them physical) instrumentation. I'd include such very powerful energies as the energy of love, the ability to recognize and appreciate beauty, inspirations originating in dreams, empathy, and many others.

I once defined love as the centripetal force that balances the centrifugal energy resulting from circular motion. This, however, only partially explains one aspect of love, which tends to unite rather than set us apart. It does not explain its empathetic aspects that, to me, remain beyond phenomenal explanation. There are people who 'give' without deriving any physical benefits from it. They even choose to remain anonymous.

Then, there is the question of knowledge. Knowledge falls into two categories: that which deals with the timeless reality of Being and that which deals with the transient reality of Becoming. Contrary to the protagonists of either side of this equation, both are of equal importance.

The knowledge of Being is fed to us from the unconscious part of our mind. The Becoming aspect is fed by the consciousness produced by our brain. While the first offers us the permanent base from which we draw on our infinite potential, the second is vital to understanding the

CONCLUSIONS

Universal Laws of Becoming.

I cannot stress too strongly that both are of equal importance. If we assign the Being aspect to religions, and forsake the manifestation of the Infinite Potential dwelling within us, we shall miss to whole purpose of life, of our being here, in the phenomenal Universe, replete with wondrous miracles. Perhaps, as so often, Albert Einstein put it into words:

> ***"Science** without **religion** is lame,*
> ***religion** without **science** is blind."*

And this applies to *all* people who attempt to fathom the mysteries of the Universal Laws. By limiting our potential, we limit our purpose and the whole purpose of the phenomenal world. To put it into more prosaic words, Being provides the potential, Becoming is intended to prove its existence. Hence, both are infinite.

There is, however, one vital act which we cannot ignore. The two coexist simultaneously. If one or the other is dormant within us, within our consciousness, then we are only half alive. Regrettably, this applies to all people who deny the Potential inherent within them. Within their Consciousness. Hence the ancient prophets' assurance, repeated by Yeshûa, that we are gods.

Gods, in this context, means only one thing. We are immortal, omnipotent, infinite and One.

Even as our physical bodies are hosts to 100 trillion microbes, so we can consider ourselves as integral members of a single entity we know not only as humanity but as all life-forms manifesting in the phenomenal reality. And this is not limited to our Earth, our solar system, our galaxy, or all the galaxies manifested in the phenomenal Multiverse; this is a hypothetical group of multiple phenomenal universes that comprise everything that exists. All phenomenal realities in the multiverse are a controlled by the same Universal Laws.

In the fullness of time we will advance our understanding of quantum entanglement, let alone quantum superimposition. Quantum entanglement allows the particles to interact simultaneously, no matter how far they are physically apart. Quantum superimposition goes even further. It suggests that particles can exist in two different location also simultaneously.

These latest scientific theories gravitate towards the Singularity of the phenomenal Universe. Even as our forefathers claimed that God is One, now we are beginning to accept that the manifestation of the Omnipresent Creative Energy, that the prophets referred to as God, is only One.

But what is even more significant is that the Energy that controls the phenomenal reality is also a Single Energy, although it appears to manifest an ability to metamorphose into the incredibly complex Universe which we can perceive with our senses. Even an in-depth study of our physical body attests to this complexity. Billions of cells abiding with trillions of microorganisms in perfect harmony. Or at least fairly perfect, if we don't abuse the Universal Laws that put us together over millions of years. In time, thanks to the energy that directs our evolution, our perception of the magnitude of these energies will grow exponentially.

This ability allows us to contribute to the expansion of 'our' Universe, that is an integral part of the Multiverse. After all, as Albert Einstein assured us,

"All is energy."

This includes us and any energies we might generate by our brain. Expansion of diversity of our Universe is a *sine qua non* Law that cannot be terminated.

Why?

Because time is a dimension of the phenomenal Universe only, which is in constant movement. The state of Being, however, is in eternal stasis.

And we, you and I, have the unique privilege of combining both, Being and Becoming.

Aren't we lucky?

TO SUM UP

Being and Becoming are two faces of the same reality: the Potential and the Execution. Mind is the energy linking the two. The expression *"Son of the living God"* simply means that we, the sons and daughters of the "living god" are spawned by the phenomenal Universe *i.e.,* the "living, eternally metamorphosing Potential in the illusory, transient reality."

Hence, in biblical symbolism, the phenomenal Universe *is* the *Living* God, as the pure, Creative Energy of Consciousness, which reduced Its rate of vibration to become perceptible to our senses. The Energy of Being continues to vibrate at an infinite rate, which is the 'God' of the Infinite Potential.

Of course, essentially, the two are One.

While the rest of nature, on Earth, conforms to the Universal Laws, *i.e.,* to the laws that control the phenomenal Universe, we, the human species, in addition to being integral part of nature, have the power to partake in the creative process of converting the Potential into *Phenomenality*. We must never forget the meaning of this word. It also means *prodigious, extraordinary,* and *exceptional*. This is what we are, and this is what our Universe is.

~~~**Prodigious, exceptional, extraordinary**~~~

PHENOMENAL

We, and the countless millennia of evolution, perhaps all eternity, have created the Universe, and we continue to create it. We are the instruments through which diversity and enhancement are added to the reality of the phenomenal world. This, and this alone, makes us *"children of the Most High"*. The children of the *"Living God."* The illusory children of the transient Universe. Yet within us there remains the indestructible, immortal, irrepressible Energy of the Creative Consciousness. In that sense, we are inseparable from the totality of the Creative Consciousness.

All else is an illusion.

When we fully unite our awareness of the two aspects of our nature, the Being and the Becoming, we become *Avatars*.

As I wrote in *DELUSIONS*, I will let you go by repeating, again, just two quotes from my favourite scientist, Albert Einstein. The first is a comment on Pragmatic Realism; the second, reflects my personal philosophy of life.

"Reality is merely an illusion, albeit a very persistent one."

"A person starts to live when he can live outside himself."

~~~

(1) M-theory is a theory in physics that unifies all consistent versions of superstring theory. The existence of such a theory was first conjectured by Edward Witten at a string theory conference at the University of Southern California in the spring of 1995.
(M-theory - Wikipedia)
(2) Panpsychism was discussed in Chapter 17.
(3) by thoughts and emotions.

APPENDIX IV
ESSENCE OF LIFE

"I... a universe of atoms, an atom in the universe." ... I don't feel frightened not knowing things, by being lost in a mysterious universe without any purpose, which is the way it really is as far as I can tell."
Richard Phillips Feynman (1918 - 1988)
American physicist,
recipient of joint Nobel Prize in Physics in 1965

...until now?

The human race persists under a great misapprehension. While evolution has equipped us with virtually immortal genes, those genes are intended to extend the longevity of our physical bodies. Under the circumstances, for as long as we identify our lives with our phenomenal bodies, we can benefit from the extensive benefits of our seeming longevity.

There are, however, *two basic problems*.

One, we are not our bodies.

And two, even if we were, our physical bodies are an inseparable part of an illusory reality. A reality that does not really exist. It is transient, ephemeral, and has a very different purpose from that which most people appear to assign to it.

Let us first define who we really are.

The only true reality is the Omnipresent Energy of Consciousness. All that appears to exist has metamorphosed, and continues to metamorphose, from this primal Energy. This is an eternal Process. Hence, in the phenomenal Universe, no matter how transient or how durable,

All is energy.

This fact has been amply confirmed by *Albert Einstein*.

We, you and I, are individualizations of this omnipresent, eternal, indestructible Creative Energy of Consciousness. Be it manifest as the conscious, the subconscious, or even the unconscious energy, it is the only energy that can and does metamorphose into innumerable, virtually infinite other energies at different rates of vibration. Some of them, we, humans, can recognize and identify with our senses.

There are countless other energies of much higher rates of vibration than those that we can, at present, perceive with our senses, or even with our electronic equipment, that add up to the reality of the phenomenal Universe.

We, the human species, are only in the early stages of the Process of Becoming. The Process we know as Life.

However, as mentioned above, we, as the individualizations of the Creative Energy that congealed by slowing down Its vibrations, are inseparable from our eternal Source. We are One, and with identical potential inherent in the Omnipresent Consciousness. A droplet of the ocean is still made up of the same energy as the ocean.

One of the problems we (humanity) face is that, over countless millions, perhaps billions of years, evolution has equipped us with a magnificent biological computer we know as the *brain*, that began to generate its own phenomenal reality. The purpose to this exercise was, is, and will continue to be, to add ***diversity*** to the phenomenal Universe. Every new rate of vibration that enhances the phenomenal Universe expands Its reality. Hence, our astrophysicists observe that our Universe expands, and does so at an ever accelerating rate. In time, our local Universe that may have began only some 13.8 billion years ago will join the phenomenal reality of what we now call the Multiverse, which is eternal.

This, too, has been confirmed by the renowned

theoretical physicist and cosmologist, *Stephen Hawking*.

Yet, we must never forget that vibrations that do not enhance and hence expand the Universe are recycled for future use. The recycling restores their original rate of vibrations. The phenomenal matrices for this process are, what the astrophysicists refer to as, the **Black Holes.**

And this brings us to the crux of the 'matter'—the crux of the reason for life, for Becoming.

The sole purpose of our transient phenomenal life, or the process of Becoming, is to contribute to the reality in which we, and all manifestations of the Creative Energy of Consciousness, enjoy our Being. Since time is a dimension of only the phenomenal reality, its influence on reality is just as transient, as illusory, as all other dimensions. Only the Creative Omnipresent Energy of Consciousness, vibrating at an infinite rate, is beyond any and all dimensions, hence of any and all limitations of the phenomenal reality.

Thus the longevity of the human or any other species is of absolutely no consequence. Once any biological or zoological individual, or the whole species, fulfills the purpose for which it was created in the phenomenal reality, its rate of vibration can metamorphose into other energies which are more likely to enhance the Universe.

This Process is eternal.

There is no death.

There is, however, a process of recycling energies which did not enhance the phenomenal Universe. This process restores the original vibrations of the spent energies and merges them with the omnipresent Source for future metamorphosis. No energy is ever wasted.

There is only the metamorphosis of the Omnipresent Consciousness. And this Process of Becoming is as eternal as the Energy of Being.

EPILOGUE

> *"If you suspect you are more than flesh and bones,
> read **Stan I.S. Law.**
> If you want to be sure, read **Stanislaw Kapuscinski.**"*
> (Anonymous email received by the author)

> *"Always blow your own trumpet,
> blowing someone else's is unhygienic."*
> **Benny Bellamacina**
> British author, songwriter, poetic humorist

My brother was at our place again, last night. In Poland we celebrate Christmas Eve, often followed by *Pasterka*, the Midnight Mass. While I no longer partake in *Pasterka*, we still celebrate the Birth of Christ as a family occasion, with carols, Christmas tree, and *Wigilia*, which is the traditional Christmas Eve vigil supper in Poland.

And for us, in Canada.

My brother is a lot younger than I am, some 16 years, yet his physical condition does not show it. He is still a PhD scientist, rejecting (to my knowledge) everything that cannot be measured or experienced in the phenomenal Universe. For him this world is real, and there is none other.

I shared the very same sentiments some time ago. Actually quite a few years have passed since I've published my

Dictionary Of Biblical Symbolism

which, after an arduous eight months research at the McGill University Library of Religious Studies, opened my own eyes as much as, apparently, many of my readers'. What opened my eyes was the discovery that the Bible has nothing to do with any religion. It is no more than a wonderful compilation of wisdom based on observations of what makes the human species happy. Men and women, of course.

In other words, it illustrates what can make one successful while here and now. Successful and happy! Not after we die, in some elusive Heaven, let alone Hell, but here and now. Yet this knowledge gathered over thousands of years is only accessible to people who will take the time and effort to understand the symbolic meaning of the scriptures. Otherwise, reading it is a waste of time.

The punch line of it all is relatively simple.

As I've written many times before, Heaven and Hell are states of Consciousness. They are not the carrot and the stick offered us by religions. They are here and now or, as reputedly Yeshûa said, they are those states of Consciousness that are *within us*.

To repeat again, *here and now*.

And we alone create both. Individually. This is what makes us gods. We have the power to create reality in which we enjoy our life.

My second conclusion was that the world of our Becoming is set on automatic. There isn't a single entity controlling our thoughts, behaviour or actions, but the eternity stretching into the past has established certain principles that work, that sustain the vitality of the reality in which we enjoy our Becoming. Einstein called them the *"Thoughts of God,"* I call them the *Universal Laws*.

If we really want to be happy in this or any other reality, then finding out what those Laws are is *sine qua non* to reach the Paradise which is here, all around us, waiting to be discovered.

All around and all within. It is omnipresent.

I have one hint to offer.

If you really want to find it, don't go looking for it far

and wide. Save your time and energy.
Look for it within.

It seems that my dear brother doesn't thinks so. He doesn't believe me. After all, no man can be a prophet in his own village. Or town. Or even in his family. Nevertheless, he is still relatively young. Perhaps, as Buddha would say, he'll awaken. One day. After all, aren't we all immortal?

(I can write freely about him because I know he'll never read any of my books. He told me as much!)

On the other hand, I admire his knowledge of physics. He didn't get his PhD for nothing!

For now, I'll leave you with this thought. If the Universe is eternal, and so is evolution, then, sooner or later, you and I will be able to create and/or destroy a planet, or at the very least all life on such a planet, with a blink of an eye.

No, this is not science-fiction.

This is the scourge of living in an eternal Universe which continues to expand for eternity. Unless we learn to love one another, to love all life, all nature, to love the reality which surrounds us, this might and—judging by our past—*will* happen.

We shall remain the immortal individualizations of the indestructible, inexhaustible, eternal Omnipotent Creative Energy. Our creation will not. In fact, as you know, our creation is only an illusion. Blame Einstein, it's his idea. And, after all, he, too, had a PhD.

Creative Energy can be used to build and/or to destroy. We metamorphose one energy to create another by slowing or increasing their vibrations. Those that don't serve us any more, we revert to the original rate of vibrations. To pure Consciousness. Look at the Black Holes. That is where the rebirth takes place, often on mega-scale. Imagine a Black Hole the size of a galaxy; or of a galactic cluster. And yet we are indivisible from our Immortal Source. As I keep saying, we are gods.

To repeat, we create our realities. And, on the other hand, we have the power to just destroy the illusions we've created... Even the very persistent ones. Remember, it's all just an illusion...

Good luck.

AND THIS IS ONLY FOR THE FEW...
...only for those who wish to heal themselves...
and others?

A few words, only for those who are ready to receive them. I'm sure there'll only be a Few...

They sum up my *Conclusions* inspired by Einstein, the Bible (the non-religious version), Evelyn Monahan and my own *Pragmatic Reality*.

Not necessarily in that order...

Please note *pragmatic* means, *inter alia*, practical, matter-of-fact, sensible, down-to-earth, having both one's feet on the ground, hardheaded, and no-nonsense.

Let us begin with **Albert Einstein**.

He said that *"A person starts to live when he can live outside himself."* He or she, of course. To be able to fulfill Einstein's advise, we must first accept that we are energy. That the material body we perceive with the physical senses generated by our brain is the product of our artificial intelligence that has its becoming in the illusory reality. That everything we perceive with any of our senses is an illusion. (Yes, this is Einstein again.) After all, hydrogen, the most abundant atom in the phenomenal Universe is

99.9999999999999% empty space. Hence, Einstein must have been right. We imagine that we see solids. They are all an illusion. The Phenomenal Universe is not only transient and illusory, but also... empty space.

Energy *is* empty space. Photons have no mass. Nor do other energies, such as thoughts, various emotions, and, most of all, Consciousness—Consciousness which mind metamorphoses into the creative energy of thoughts.

Why? Because the only true reality is the Omnipresent Consciousness. (Remember how real your dreams are while you're dreaming?) The Consciousness that individualizes Itself into each and every one of us, into all flora and fauna, into every single atom and subatomic particle.

Though metamorphosed through different rates of vibrations into an infinite number of different energies, ultimately Consciousness is the only reality.

So much for Albert.

Next, we move to the wisdom of the past, *i.e.,* the **Bible**. This is a veritable goldmine of information that remains ignored for countless generations by most people. For our purposes, we must look at the two, probably the most overlooked, sentences in the Bible. Sentences that at first sight do not seem to make any sense.

> *"Be ye perfect even as your father is perfect."* (Matthew 5:48)

> *"Thou art of purer eyes than to behold evil, and canst not look on iniquity..."* (Habakkuk 2:13)

This is either complete nonsense or there is wisdom there that applies to us. Have you ever heard of anyone that was perfect? And yet... this statement appears to apply to *all* of us. Surely, it cannot apply to our illusory body, or character, or even emotional potential. Hence, the statement addresses something other than us.

Who then?

It applies to our... real selves? Our Higher Selves? But aren't they perfect already?

So... that leaves only our illusory selves... It must be a reference to our Egos, our phenomenal selves generated by our brains that are intended to be, or are to become, as perfect as our Higher Selves?

They must have been kidding, right... and yet?

Apparently.

And then there is this business about not beholding evil... or not becoming aware of iniquity...

This would work only if the reality we live in wasn't real. If it was but an illusion. A transient sham. What was it that Einstein had said about it?

So, let us get this straight. We are not to recognize imperfection in anyone or anything yet, at the same time, be perfect ourselves. Well, dear friends. This cannot happen in the reality we recognize as real. It could only happen in our imagination... or our consciousness?

And so... if we perceive imperfection it is not real? It is no more than an illusion?

Like Einstein said...?

And this brings us to **Evelyn Monahan**.

> *"How do I love thee? Let me count the ways."*
> **Elizabeth Barrett Browning.**

Elizabeth Browning's Sonnet seems comparable to Evelyn Monahan's practically euphoric admiration of our physical bodies. *"My mind and body are so magnificently constructed* *that no feat of engineering could ever duplicate the uniqueness in myself."*

Hardly surprising... Just listen to a few facts about the flabbergasting complexity with which evolution endowed us for our temporary abode. It seems, to me, that such miraculous diversity could only have been guided by the Omnipresent Consciousness:

A typical human body of some 70 kg consists of seven billion billion billion atoms. That's a 7 followed by 27 zeros.

7,000,000,000,000,000,000,000,000,000.

A nice round figure, though I have no idea who counted them...

Of these 2/3 are hydrogen (mostly empty space), the rest with oxygen and carbon add up to 99% of the total. (still mostly also empty space).

These make up an average of 37.2 trillion cells.

Not to be outdone, we are hosts to a 100 trillion microbes that inhabit just about every part of our body, probably also made up of mostly empty space.

Of the 37.2 trillion cells, our nervous system consists of some 86 billion neurons, which specialize in carrying messages through an electrochemical process.

What feeds energy into the whole system is blood, which is oxygenated in our lungs. In the adult human body of the total number of cells, 20 to 30 trillion are red blood cells, which are approximately 70% of all cells. According to the National Heart Blood Lung Institute of the Institutes of Health, the heart continuously pumps oxygen and nutrient-rich blood throughout our bodies. This is accomplished by some 100,000 beats per day pumping 5 to 6 quarts of blood each minute, which adds up to about 2,000 gallons each day. To oxygenate this blood, we take, when at rest, some 17,000 to 30,000 breaths every day. A lot more when we're active.

And then there are eleven major organ systems. They include the circulatory, respiratory, digestive, excretory, nervous, endocrine, immune, integumentary (that's hair, nails and suchlike), skeletal, muscle, and reproductive systems. The last one is a lot more than just sex.

And all these systems function harmoniously, without our conscious participation. Do you still think that you are smart enough to do it all by yourself? Or is there a higher, a *much* higher intelligence guiding, coordinating, and harmonizing it all for the sole purpose of giving us the pleasure of Becoming? The pleasure of life.

How about Omnipresent Consciousness?

I think Evelyn Monahan has a point. We really are *"magnificent human beings... without equal in all creation..."*

Please, let us not waste the miracles of our bodies.

~~~~

And yet... there are 'imperfections', mostly caused by our ignorance. We are still evolving, and will continue to evolve... forever?

After all, our potential is infinite.

Such is our reality that only our physical senses—those generated and supported by the artificial intelligence, again, generated by our (albeit) magnificent brain, can become aware of the illusion of our phenomenal reality. The true reality that is perceived by our Higher Self can only be aware of perfection. Hence, the illusory reality of the phenomenal world is, by definition, illusory, wherein, if we could only regard it with our Higher Consciousness, we would see only the truth. The perfect potential.

Hence, to 'cure' any malady all we need do is to see the truth that forever remains perfect. All else if but an illusion.

As already mentioned, I have a little book authored by

Evelyn Monahan, *The Miracle of Metaphysical Healing*. I've already described her problems and cures in previous chapters (see Chapters 1 and 3). But there is one thing I didn't mention.

After she'd given up on the inept medical profession and took matters into her own hands, it took some ten days before the cure occurred. But, and this is very important, when it did happen, it was instantaneous. There was no gradual improvement in her condition. One moment she was blind, the next she could see. The same happened with her other problems.

In her affirmations of successful healing, she also added:

"I will transcend all ordinary thinking and dwell entirely in my higher self."

We must realize that she was as new to "metaphysical healing" as any one of us would be, should we need it. And, as though the above weren't enough, she added, apparently to strengthen her resolve:

"In the awareness of my higher self I know no limits. My will is the strongest force in all of creation. I will now to be in ever-increasing contact with my higher self."

I don't know about you, but in my ears I hear silent echoes of *"I and my father are one."*

Obviously there was no healing period. There was only diametric change in her perception of reality. I'd suggest that she practiced what has been preached, and ignored, for generations. She managed to convince herself that she could see. She refused to see imperfection, rejected it completely and, even as she was reiterating her faith in the power of energized mind, and the infinite knowledge of her Higher

Self, she thanked It for the cure as though it had already happened.

Of course, she always was perfect. Aren't we all individualizations of the Omnipresent Consciousness?

Of the Eternal Perfect Potential?

And, my dear friends, her 'method' did work. It did happen. There is an incredible power in the faith. She called it the miracle of metaphysical healing, where as, in fact, *she simply refused to accept imperfection*. To do so, she had learned to regard herself not with her physical eyes but through the perception of her Higher Self.

The Higher Self, the Individualization of the Omnipresent Consciousness, that cannot behold evil. Or even imperfection!

The wondrous thing is that Habakkuk knew this around the 7th century BC. And we, the advanced *homo sapience*, have lost the wisdom of our forefathers.

Isn't it time we woke up?

Just one more detail.

We didn't get kicked out of the Garden of Eden. Of Paradise. Adam and Eve did. We can still enjoy the illusive reality of the Paradise of the Phenomenal Universe, that enhances our Becoming, as Adam and Eve had for a timeless while. We can still spend our lives in the Gardens of our own making. This is what the Age of Aquarius is for. For our awakening in the transient reflection of our Inner Perfection.

This is my Pragmatic Reality.

Welcome to my world.

Smashwords wrote in their Annual Review:

If you write a book that touches your readers' soul, or inspires them with passion or knowledge, your readers will market your book for you.

I've done my part. The rest is up to you.

BIBLIOGRAPHY

[This includes the original Bibliography of *"DELUSIONS—Pragmatic Realism"* (which may be useful for people who have not yet read the first volume), and added a few extra references. *"CONCLUSIONS—Pragmatic Reality"* leans heavily on the same bibliography which influenced the previous book.]

Arnold, Sir Edwin, M.A., K.C.I.E., C.S.I., *The Song Celestial or Bhagavad Gita,* (Self-Realization Fellowship, LA.).

Bryson, Bill, *The Body*, (Doubleday Canada).

Black, Margaret J. *Freud and Beyond* (Harper Collins).

Blavatsky, H.P., (An Abridgement of) *The Secret Doctrine*, (The Theosophical Publishing House).

Evelyn M. Monahan *The Miracle of Metaphysical Healing*, (1975, Parker Publishing Co. New York).

Green, Brian, *The Elegant Universe*, (Vintage Books, Random House, Inc. New York).

Campbell, Joseph, *The Hero with a Thousand Faces*, (Bollingen Series XVII, Princeton University Press).

Dawkins, Richard, *Climbing Mount Improbable,* (W.W. Norton & Co., New York, London)

Dawkins, Richard, *The God Delusion,* (Houghton Mifflin Harcourt)

Feynman, Richard P., *Surely you're joking, Mr. Feynman!* (A Bantam Book)

Follett, Ken, *Fall of Giants,* (Pan Macmillan)

Fouts, Roger and Tukel Mills, Stephen, *Next of Kin: My conversations with Chimpanzees,* (William Morrow Paperbacks)

Hacker, Randi, *Close Call 1: Survival of the Fittest,* ebook, (Smashwords Edition).

Imperial Reference Bible, King James Version, (Thomas Nelson Inc.).

Kapuscinski, Stanislaw, *Beyond Religion I, Essay #52,* ebook, Inhousepress, (Amazon/Kindle and Smashwords).

Kapuscinski, Stanislaw, *Beyond Religion II, Fundamentalism,*

Spirit, ebook, Inhousepress, (Amazon/Kindle and Smashwords).

Kapuscinski, Stanislaw, *Beyond Religion III, The Green Eyed Monster, Church,* ebook, Inhousepress, (Amazon/Kindle and Smashwords).

Kapuscinski, Stanislaw, *Key to Immortality;* Commentary on the Gospel of Thomas, ebook, Inhousepress, (Amazon/Kindle and Smashwords).

Kapuscinski, Stanislaw, *Dictionary of Biblical Symbolism,* ebook, Inhousepress, (Amazon/Kindle and Smashwords).

Kapuscinski, Stanislaw, *VISUALIZATION—Creating Your Own Universe,* ebook, Inhousepress, (Amazon/Kindle and Smashwords).

Kapuscinski, Stanislaw, *DELUSIONS — Pragmatic Realism*, (Amazon/Kindle and Smashwords).

Krishnamurti, J., *Exploration into Insight*, (Harper & Row).

Jayakar Pupul, *Krishnamurti*, a biography, (Harper & Row).

Kurzweil, Ray, *The Singularity is Near*, (Viking, Penguin Group).

Lao-Tzu, *Tao Te Ching*, Transl. by D. Lau, (Alfred A. Knopf).

Lederman, Leon, with Teresi, Dick, *The God Particle*, (Houghton Mifflin Company).

Monahan, Evelyn, M., *The Miracle of Metaphysical Healing,* (Prentice Hall Trade).

Pearson, Carol S. Ph.D., *The Hero Within*, (Harper Collins).

Prabhupada, A.C. Bhaktivedanta Swami, *Bhagavad-Gita, As It Is*, (The Bhaktivedanta Book Trust).

Siddhartha Mukherjee in *The Gene: An Intimate History,* (Scribner; Reprint edition)

The Nag Hammadi Library, The definitive new translation of the Gnostic scriptures, James M. Robinson, General Editor, (Harper San Francisco).

Tippler, Franks, *Physics of Immortality,* (Anchor Books, Doubleday).

Twitchell, Paul, *Shariyat-Ki-Sugmad*, Illuminated Wary Press.

Venter, J. Craig, *A Life Decoded*, (Penguin Books).

Waldrop, M. Mitchell, *Complexity—The Emerging science at the edge of Order and Chaos*, (Touchstone Book, Simon & Shuster).

Watson, Lyall, *Lightning Bird,* (Hodder and Stoughton Ltd, Coronet edition).

Acknowledgments

I would be remiss were I not to thank my many friends for their comments, advice, and proofreading. As always my gratitude to my wife, Bozena Happach, who put up with being a grass widow for weeks on end, and then offered me her inspired insights. To her this book is dedicated.

*Sincerely,
Stanisław Kapuściński*

A Word about the Author

Stanislaw Kapuscinski, (aka **Stan I.S. Law**), architect, sculptor and prolific writer, was educated in Poland and England. Since 1965 he has resided in Canada. His special interests cover a broad spectrum of arts, sciences and philosophy. His fiction and non-fiction attest to his particular passion for the scope and the development of Human Potential. He has authored more than forty books, twenty of them novels.

Under his real name he has published eighteen non-fiction books sharing his vision of reality. He has also composed two collections of poems in his original native tongue in which he satirizes his view of the world while paying homage to Bozena Happach's sculptures.

INHOUSEPRESS INTERVIEW

As a youngster, Stanislaw Kapuscinski, aka Stan I.S. Law, studied the violin. By the time he reached the age of 16, he had played (rather badly compared to more talented youngsters) some violin concertos. Beethoven's in E, opus 61, was his favourite. In Sibelius, Mendelssohn, let alone Paganini, he claimed to have mastered only the Andante movements. But what mattered was that he evidently developed an abiding love for what is now known as Classical Music.

To add insult to injury, (injury being the noise generated by the vast majority of today's 'musicians') the moment his voice broke from boyish falsetto to *basso cantante*, often called bass-baritone, he fell in love with opera—all this while studying architecture.

The next ten years he studied a variety of operatic roles,

while continuing with the violin and architecture. He confessed that by the time he turned 50 or so, he began to give up on television. The noise the so-called composers produced to accompany, if not drown, the dialogues of the inept TV actors, who never took a single lesson in elocution, disgusted him on both counts. He realized that perversion of music (remember "Music of the Spheres") became the scourge of our times. He claims that it is no longer music. That it is an abysmal dissonance. A disruptive noise. A cacophony of electric guitars and percussion. Occasionally, he said, he'd switch on TV without sound and watch while making up his own story to match the actor's behaviour. He insisted that the stories he made up were bound to be better than whatever the TV noise could generate.

To his further chagrin, he claimed that other art forms registered a similar downward spiral.

Luckily, there were, there always are, the Few. The select Few who don't follow the dictates or the tastes of (what he calls) the "Third Party". Of the vast majority.

For a while, architecture sated his need for creative effort. He designed dozens of buildings, including multi-storied headquarters for a number of companies. And then, the inevitable happened. As politics in the province to which he had emigrated from Europe changed, so did his firm's ability to get new contracts. The firm went bankrupt.

"Now", he said, "you know why I'm writing."

So far, since he retired from his profession, the bankruptcy has resulted in forty-five books. This is the forty-sixth.

Who knows where the silent voice will take him next. Perhaps, he'll take up painting? Whatever it is, I'm sure he'll imbue it with all the passion that characterizes all his other endeavours.

He blames the silent voice for that.

The silent voice within.

By the same author

Non-fiction
(Most are available as e-books and paperback format).

VISUALIZATION—Creating your own Universe
KEY TO IMMORTALITY
[Commentary on the Gospel of Thomas]
BEYOND RELIGION Volume I
BEYOND RELIGION Volume II
BEYOND RELIGION Volume III
[Each volume contains 52 Essays on Perception of Reality]
DICTIONARY OF BIBLICAL SYMBOLISM
PSALM 23 [Interpretation]
VICIOUS CIRCLE, (Volumes 1 to 6)
[In search of Secular Ethics]
DELUSIONS—Pragmatic Realism
CONCLUSIONS—Pragmatic Reality
PSALM 23—In Search of Secular Ethics
ISAIAH (9:6)—In Search of Secular Ethics
LORD'S PRAYER—In Search of Secular Ethics
DECALOGUE—In Search of Secular Ethics

Fiction by Stan I.S. Law
(aka Stanislaw Kapuscinski)
Novels

WALL—Love, Sex and Immortality [Aquarius Trilogy Book I]
PLUTO EFFECT [Aquarius Trilogy Book II]
OLYMPUS — Of Gods and Men [Aquarius Trilogy Book III]
MARVIN CLARK—In Search of Freedom
GIFT OF GAMMAN
ENIGMA OF THE SECOND COMING
ONE JUST MAN [Winston Trilogy Book I]
ELOHIM—Masters & Minions [Winston Trilogy Book II]
WINSTON'S KINGDOM [Winston Trilogy Book III]
THE AVATAR SYNDROME [prequel to Headless World]
HEADLESS WORLD [Sequel to The Avatar Syndrome]
THE PRINCESS [Alexander Trilogy Book I]

ALEXANDER [Alexander Trilogy Book II]
SACHA—The Way Back [Alexander Trilogy Book III]
YESHUA—Personal Memoir of the Missing Years of Jesus
THE GATE—Things my Mother told Me
NOW—Being and Becoming
ALEXANDER TRILOGY
AVATAR TRILOGY
AQUARIUS TRILOGY
WINSTON TRILOGY

Anthologies of Short Stories

THE JEWEL
CATS and DOGS Series
SCI-FI 1
SCI-FI 2

Poetry in Polish

KILKA SŁÓW I TROCHĘ GLINY
WIĘCEJ SŁÓW I WIĘCEJ GLINY

Your comments are very welcome.
Please write your reviews/comments
wherever you acquired your copy.
Your thoughts are important to us.
Thanks.

INHOUSEPRESS

www.ingramcontent.com/pod-product-compliance
Lightning Source LLC
Chambersburg PA
CBHW022354040426
42450CB00005B/174